The Good Shepherd

Also by Jo Coudert

Seven Cats and the Art of Living

GoWell: The Story of a House

The Alcoholic in Your Life

Advice from a Failure

I Never Cooked Before Cookbook

With Yvonne S. Thornton, M.D.

Woman to Woman

The Ditchdigger's Daughters

The Good Shepherd

A Special Dog's Gift of Healing

Jo Coudert

Andrews McMeel Publishing
Kansas City

 For information, write Andrews McMeel Publishing, an Andrews McMeel Universal company, 4520 Main Street, Kansas City, Missouri 64111.

www.andrewsmcmeel.com

98 99 00 01 02 RDH 10 9 8 7 6 5 4 3 2

Library of Congress Cataloging-in-Publication Data

Coudert, Jo.
The good shepherd : a special dog's gift of healing / Jo Coudert.
p. cm.
ISBN 0-8362-6756-7 (hd)
1. Dogs--Therapeutic use. 2. Davis, Lana. 3. Schmaling, Jeremy, 1972- . I. Title.
RM931.D63C68 1998 98-22466
636.7'088--dc21 CIP

Some names have been changed in the text to protect the privacy of the people involved.

For
Jeremy, Lana, and Grizzly
with admiration

Contents

Foreword

by Susan McElroy

My first book, *Animals as Teachers and Healers,* was composed of a wide selection of brief anecdotes about people whose lives had been healed, touched, or transformed by an animal. What I was *not* able to provide in the format of that book was the rich, time-treasured view of a life lived in the company of a special animal companion through many years and many challenges. *The Good Shepherd* fills that void beautifully and courageously in the story of Lana Davis, her son, Jeremy, and their beloved dog, Grizzly.

Do not be fooled into believing that this is merely a book about a brave boy, a mother with a fierce and tender heart, and their uncannily intelligent dog. It is, of course, about these things but, more important, it is about relationships and about healing. *The Good Shepherd* teaches us just how broad and strong and miraculous the horizon of relationships can be when we include animals in the mix as friends, family, and—yes—as mentors and healers.

As a cancer survivor, I discovered early in the process of my illness that there is a distinct difference between curing and healing. *Curing* means that all physical traces of the disease go away. By *healing,* I mean coming into a greater state of wholeness in body, mind, and soul. Healing, I have come to believe, is needed on many levels, regardless of one's physical condition. Hearts need healing. Relationships need healing. Overwhelmed spirits and tired souls need healing. When I was ill, I understood that while a cure for my cancer might have been beyond my grasp, healing was something I could participate in, no matter what my physical state. Now, medical science is acknowledging that any and all emotional healing impacts actual physical healing as well.

When people ask me how animals can serve as healers, I tell them that a dog may not be able to bandage your wounds or cure you of an illness, but the lessons a dog can teach us about healing are legion. In the loss of her young son to cancer, Lana Davis endured one of life's most horrible tragedies. That her healing came to her on four feet, in the form of a devoted dog who simply would not let her give up on life, is just one example of how animals can lead us to greater states of wellness. This same dog, Grizzly, stood vigil over her dying son, offering him round-the-clock comfort and companionship. No one can measure what Grizzly's devotion may have meant to Jeremy or chart what psychological or spiritual healing may well have transpired between them.

Lana's story of *The Good Shepherd* is powerful, and it is genuine. Anyone who has ever loved and lived with an animal cannot doubt its authenticity. Yet our culture continues to diminish and dismiss the value of animals in our lives. People who work with animals are often asked, "Shouldn't you devote your time to more important causes?" Those of us who love animals are often told we should spend our precious love on people instead—as though there were a finite supply of love and we are wasting a scarce resource. Everywhere we look, animals are portrayed as "less than." This kind of cultural conditioning breaks my heart. How many gifted healers in animal skins have we failed to acknowledge in our lives because of this "less than" mentality?

Lana's story begins with a great loss close to her heart. It grows into a gift of love and healing to her community. Along the way—in anecdotes startling in their freshness and creativity—Grizzly and many other four-legged creatures answer the question, "How do animals heal us?" By the time you have finished this book, I can guarantee that you will never again doubt the intangible, awesome abilities of animal healers. Open your vision wide, and let your personal definitions of "relationship" and "healing" expand to include all of creation. You, and all the world, will be the better for it.

Part I

If Something Ends

1
The Fateful Future

The German shepherd padded down the hospital corridor, pausing almost imperceptibly at each door in case there might be a tug on his leash to tell him to turn in. "No, Grizzly," Lana said, "we're heading home now." On this, their first visit to the hospital, Lana did not want to jeopardize their success by having the dog perhaps lose patience with the children, although the shepherd gave no sign of feeling stressed.

A nurse came out of a room down the hall. She closed the door and sagged against it before stiffening her shoulders and glancing up. Catching sight of the dog and his partner, she suddenly looked hopeful. "Oh, please," she said, hurrying to them. "This must be Grizzly. Could you . . . would you . . . ?"

Lana shook her head. Their hour in the hospital was up; they were on their way out. But she listened as the nurse explained that in the room she had just left there was an eleven-year-old girl named Shelley who that morning had been given a terminal diagnosis. Her parents were even now talking to the doctors to see if there wasn't something, anything, that could be done. Meanwhile, Shelley's older brother was with her, trying to comfort her, trying to persuade her to eat, something she had not done in days.

Before this crushing news had come, the children had heard that Grizzly was expected and had been looking forward to meeting him. Even now, a visit from Grizzly might help.

"Well," Lana murmured doubtfully.

"Please."

The nurse had been walking with them, and now she quietly opened the door of the room to give Lana a glimpse of the children. The little girl, shadowy in her frailness, was clinging to her brother and crying, her back to the door. On her brother's face was written his own pain and fear, his sense of helplessness, of not knowing how to make it through this moment, and the next, and the next. It was a look that Lana had seen on the faces of her daughters two years before. The boy was about fifteen, sixteen at the most, Jeremy's age, but forever now he would be older than his years, Lana knew, and she grieved for him, for his sister, and for her own lost son.

The boy heard the click of Grizzly's toes on the floor as the dog took a step forward. "Shelley," he said, cupping his hand under his little sister's chin, "Shelley, look who's here. It's the dog. It's Grizzly!"

"Grizzly?" The dark-eyed girl, tearstained and with translucent skin as pale as white flour, wheeled. "Oh, Grizzly!" She dropped to the floor as Grizzly moved to her, and her arms went around his neck. She buried her face in his ruff, sobbing against him as she had been crying against her brother. Lana sat down on the floor beside them, saying nothing, just letting Grizzly be with Shelley for whatever comfort his even breathing and beating heart might give her. Grizzly was quiet for a time; then rumbles, as various as though they were words, began deep in his throat.

"He's talking to me," Shelley marveled. Unexpectedly, she giggled. Grizzly revved up his orchestra of sounds. Shelley laughed aloud. She lifted her face to Lana.

"What's he saying? Is he saying he's hungry?"

"I don't think so," Lana told her. "He had his breakfast, and he's not used to eating again until suppertime." But Shelley had already pulled herself up and was reaching for her untouched lunch tray.

Lana added hastily, "Anyway, he doesn't like people food."

Shelley was adamant. "I think he's saying he's hungry. I'm going to feed him my lunch." On the tray was a turkey sandwich with lettuce, sliced tomatoes, onion, and pickles. Lana prayed that Shelley would offer Grizzly the turkey from the sandwich; he might eat that. Instead, Shelley held out a piece of lettuce. Grizzly gravely sniffed it, plucked it from her hand, and after a preliminary munch swallowed it. "See, he *is* hungry!" Shelley crowed.

He's not hungry and he does not eat lettuce, Lana thought. But there was no way of knowing that from Grizzly's behavior. He cocked his head expectantly as Shelley picked up a slice of pickle.

"You want this pickle, don't you?" Shelley said, and Grizzly accepted it from her fingers as though it were a succulent piece of liver. "What else is there? Turkey. Ah, I can eat that. And a piece of bread. You can have the tomato. I don't like tomatoes. Do you like tomatoes, Grizzly?"

"Woof," said Grizzly, as convincingly as though tomatoes were a dog's favorite food.

Shelley continued to pick the food apart, a bite for her, a bite for Grizzly, while Grizzly mimed that he had never tasted anything so delicious, including the slice of onion. Shelley, swallowing the first solid food she had had in days, announced that it tasted good and could she have some more? The nurse and Shelley's brother both had tears in their eyes, for, as the nurse told Lana when they left, the doctors had been about to resort to forced feeding through a nasogastric tube to get some essential nourishment into Shelley. Grizzly had accomplished what no human being had been able to do.

"Thank you," the nurse added, following Lana into the hall. "You and Grizzly have made all the difference."

Suddenly the boy was there beside them, leaning down to hug Grizzly. "I never expected to hear Shelley laugh again," he whispered, and fled down the hall to hide his tears.

Lana was desperate to rush Grizzly out of the hospital before he threw up his unusual meal, so she bypassed the elevator and hurried him down the stairs. The dog had a chronic digestive problem and eating anything but lamb and rice made him ill. Once outside, Grizzly took an interest in some flowers and made a feint at a robin sipping at a rain puddle but gave no sign of being discomfited by the odd mixture in his stomach. Even the ride home in the car did not jar loose the pickles, onion, and tomato; all agreed with him seemingly quite as well as did lamb and rice.

At home, Lana went directly to the phone to call her friend Ella Brown five hundred miles away. Ella raised German shepherds, and she had known Grizzly from the time he was born. Briefly, Lana described what had happened, ending with, "Ella, Grizzly ate all that stuff! He put on this big act, as if he liked it!"

Ella laughed. "And it didn't even make him sick, I'll bet."

"It didn't! Can you believe it? This is a dog who sniffs four times before he deigns to accept a biscuit."

"Grizzly knew the little girl needed to eat."

"Ella, he's a dog! How could a dog know that?"

Ella turned serious. "Growing up with Jeremy taught Grizzly that his purpose in life was to be a caretaker, so each time he encounters someone who's sick, he figures out what they need. Just like he figured out that the right thing for you was to walk in the fields where the wind and the sun could heal you."

After she hung up, Lana made herself a cup of tea and sat at the kitchen table, looking out at the austere Wasatch Range that marched down the side of the Utah valley but remembering Ella's place in Oregon and the March day she had first taken Jeremy there.

"Jeremy," she had said, knocking quietly on the half-open door of his room, "I'm going to drive out to the kennel to pick up Sadie." Sadie was the family's cocker spaniel.

Jeremy, in blue jeans and sagging athletic socks, was lying face down on his bed. "Sure, Mom. I'll be all right."

"I know you will, sweetie." Because fingers can often talk tenderness better than words, Lana crossed to Jeremy's side and lightly rubbed his still-strong shoulders.

A piercing shaft of sunlight coming through the dormer window in the boy's bedroom swept over his shelf of trophies, picking out the crouching, speeding, chrome figure of a motorcyclist and next to it a silver cup proclaiming Jeremy Pacific Northwest Junior Karate Champion. Lana let her gaze wander over the awards and then travel on to where the sunlight deadened in the dark cotton scarf tightly looped around Jeremy's head. A few short months before, the sun would have burnished the astonishing white-gold hair that seemed to hold him in the light wherever he went. But that was before and this was after.

She said aloud, "Chrissie'll be home from school pretty soon."

"Sure."

"You can play video games."

"I tell her she should be going out for soccer."

Lana smiled. "She'll still do whatever you say, except not be with you if she can." Jeremy made a small sound that could mean *yes, no,* or *maybe,* perhaps even *I'm not up for talking,* and ordinarily Lana would not have pressed him, for he was a boy well on his way to being a man, clear-sighted and so steeped in the karate philosophy of egolessness that he had none of the usual adolescent bravado, no need to create issues or to distance himself. But she sensed Jeremy was fighting depression and she wanted to help. "There was a new litter of puppies the last time I was at the kennel," she said. "German shepherds. Ella Brown raises them."

"Really?" Life came into Jeremy's voice, for shepherds were the breed of dog he most admired.

"Maybe you'd like to go with me to get Sadie," Lana suggested. Jeremy grinned at her as he rolled over and reached for his shirt. "You knew German shepherds would get me, didn't you?"

When Lana pulled the car around to the front of the house, Jeremy was waiting on his crutches, not hunched and resting on them but standing determinedly straight, pretending he did not need their support, even though he dared not touch his left foot to the ground. On the ride to the kennel through the countryside near Klamath Falls, Oregon, where they lived, he played a tape of Christian rock and softly beat time on his knee to what he called his power music. It was clear that, as Lana had hoped, the prospect of seeing the puppies was cheering him.

When they pulled into the drive at the kennel, five dignified black-and-tan German shepherds swung smoothly to their feet and advanced in silence to meet them. The dogs were neither hostile nor friendly, merely going about their job of checking out the visitors. Jeremy took his hands off the crossbars of his crutches and turned them palm outward to reassure the dogs that the crutches were not weapons, but no dog approached to be petted until Ella emerged from the kennel office. A small woman with energy packed into her compact form and warmth in her dark eyes, she met the inquiring look of the lead dog and wordlessly signaled that these were friends. Only then did the dogs crowd around them. Lana grew concerned that they might nudge Jeremy off balance, but they delicately avoided the crutches as they searched his face to judge the meaning of the pleasant nothings he was saying to them.

Sadie, their own dog, exuberant at seeing them, was far more of a hazard to Jeremy when Ella released the cocker spaniel from her pen. Lana swooped up the ecstatically barking, squirming dog and carried her back to the car. She stayed with her a bit to kiss her muzzle and tug her soft ears, the way Sadie liked, and tell her they had missed her too; then she rejoined Ella and Jeremy. They had seated themselves in the sun on a bench outside the kennel office, with the adult dogs ranged in a semicircle around them and a tumbling heap of puppies wrestling at their feet. One puppy yelped in startled pain and Jeremy plucked it from under an attacking sibling and cradled it in his arms, stroking it into contentment while asking Ella Brown questions about the breeding of the dogs. Ella answered his queries thoughtfully, as though talking shop with a fellow breeder, with no hint that a hundred more pressing tasks undoubtedly awaited her that afternoon. She described how she bred her shepherds first for temperament, next for intelligence, and only last for conformation. But, then, even as a breeder of show dogs, she could afford to rank intelligence and temperament first, she admitted, because with the von Braun line of champions she raised, conformation was virtually a given.

"Look there." She touched Jeremy's arm to guide his attention as one of the big dogs growled warningly and reached to give a puppy a light nip. "That's the puppy's mother and she is disciplining him because he got too close to Rainy Ridge, the alpha dog. The puppy has to learn respect and his proper place in the pack." Ella turned to look briefly at Jeremy before bending her wise and patient gaze back on the dogs. "Have you ever raised a puppy?" she asked.

"We had Gretchen when I was little. She was a German shepherd but she was full-grown and I don't remember much about her except lying on the floor with my arms around her."

"Raising a puppy of your own can be a special experience, sort of like raising a child if you put enough of yourself into it and care about doing it right."

Jeremy lowered his face to the puppy in his arms, snuffling its pink, almost hairless belly. "Someday," he said, "someday when I'm able to get a job and earn money, I'm going to buy a shepherd puppy." His tone changed and he added with a glint of humor, "I expect it'll have to be a pretty darned good job before I'll be able to afford a puppy of yours, Ella. The von Braun line is awesome."

Ella nodded in matter-of-fact acknowledgment that her dogs were expensive. "I have a book that tells just about everything you need to know about German shepherds—what to look for in a puppy, how to train it, what to expect. Would you like to borrow it?" Jeremy thanked her but said that with his trips to the hospital he was not able to do much reading. "No problem," Ella said. "You can keep it as long as you want to."

Touched by her kindness, Lana volunteered to fetch the book and Ella told her where to find it in the office. At first Lana thought Ella must have misplaced it because she was searching for an ordinary book and was surprised to discover, when she finally located it, that it was coffee-table size and lavishly illustrated. Most people would have considered it far too expensive a book to loan to a boy, yet Ella had offered it unhesitatingly.

Did she know Jeremy's story? Lana tried to remember if she had mentioned it to Ella and decided it was unlikely because she was always in a last-minute rush when she dropped Sadie off at the kennel. But there had been articles in the local paper and Ella probably knew it from them.

It was a story that began the previous fall when Jeremy entered high school and the coach of the varsity football team suggested that he come out for practice with the juniors and seniors because he was a swift runner and unusually well-coordinated for a fifteen-year-old. On an October afternoon, on a hard field, Jeremy leaped to pull in a soaring pass. A tackler slammed him to the ground. Slowly, his left leg refusing his weight, the left side of his pelvis blazing with pain, Jeremy struggled to get up again. Teammates supported him to the sidelines. Through gritted teeth, Jeremy told the coach, "I guess that's it for me today."

"Are you all right? Do you need someone to drive you home?"

"It's okay. My mom'll stop by for me on her way from the dojo."

The dojo was a karate studio in downtown Klamath Falls. Nine years earlier, divorced and needing a way to support her three children—Jeremy, his older sister, Susanne, and his younger sister, Christen—Lana was working part-time in a store selling pianos when a man with burnished skin and the wood smell of a newly sharpened pencil clinging to him came in to inquire about piano lessons. The man, Roger Stewart, was a timber faller working for Weyerhaeuser in the vast stands of fir and pine around Klamath Falls. Lana would have had no trouble guessing this because it was a common occupation in that part of the country, but she intuited something uncommon in the grace of his strength and the tranquillity of his manner. It interested and puzzled her until he mentioned that his time for piano lessons might be a bit awkward because after his workday and on weekends he taught karate. That explained his ease, Lana decided. Even more, it explained how he could seem so masculine without having, in voice or walk or roll of his shoulders, an insistent macho quality. The secure masculinity without swagger was attractive. It was something she would wish for her six-year-old son to grow into, which led to her offering to give the man piano lessons if in return he would give Jeremy karate lessons.

"You've got a deal," Roger Stewart said, and shook her hand a little longer than absolutely necessary to seal the bargain.

Lana, looking on from the sidelines while Jeremy was in karate class, quickly became fascinated by the beautifully balanced, flowing movements of the ancient, rigorous form of Shorin-Ryu Karate Do that Roger Stewart taught. It was a form of karate that had originated in Okinawa, and the movements were as commandingly possessive of space as those of a ballet dancer. She was intrigued, too, by the philosophy of control of the egotistic self that was an integral part of the teaching. Before her marriage, Lana had been an accomplished pianist and violinist, and before the arrival of her children claimed her time she had also trained horses. In Shorin-Ryu, she saw an opportunity to exert the same kind of discipline over herself that her musical training and horsemanship had required. From karate she could learn to respond smoothly and strongly to subtle clues from others, to be in command of herself as she had been in command of her musical instruments and the strength of the horse. Wanting this not for reasons of pride or power but for the chance to be able to relax into wholeness and goodness, she sought Roger out and bartered for lessons for herself as well.

Whether she or Roger had gotten the best of the barter arrangement was a point of good-natured disagreement between them in the following years. Lana, in time, became one of the few women ever to earn a black belt and certification as an instructor in the Shorin-Ryu system, while Roger, with more music in his soul than in his fingers, scarcely got beyond the first book of piano exercises.

"Ah, but you got a wife and three incomparable children," Lana would remind him in rebuttal, for it was not long before they married and Roger became stepfather to Susanne, Christen, and Jeremy. It was when Lana mentioned Jeremy's name that Roger had to capitulate laughingly to her argument, for the relationship of stepson and stepfather glistened with successes. Roger could not have asked for a more apt karate pupil, and Jeremy, in the tradition of Shorin-Ryu, which directs the more advanced pupils to teach the less advanced, soon was functioning as an instructor as well as pupil.

Karate was only one of the skills that Roger taught Jeremy. The boy learned to operate heavy machinery, to fell trees and snake them out of the woods, but more than that, he became as attuned to animals and nature as an Indian, for Roger taught him to walk lightly on the earth and to cherish it by being alert to its wonders. He taught the boy always to remember that actions have consequences and to stay as aware of his everyday actions as he was of his karate moves. He taught him to labor hard and responsibly. Because he rode a Yamaha FJ1100, as fast a bike as was on the road, after seriously schooling Jeremy in safety, he outfitted him in a helmet and leathers and taught him to race minibikes on an indoor track. While coaching Jeremy in the skills necessary to win, he instilled in him the martial arts philosophy: Winning is not the goal, beating competitors is not the goal, the goal, simply, is always to do one's best. Because inherent in that is the implication that every other competitor is also doing his best, and because a personal best is all that can reasonably be expected of anyone, Jeremy learned the difficult lesson never to revel in a sense of conquest, never to gloat, always to honor others' efforts. Lana was particularly grateful to Roger for that because winning came easily to Jeremy and he might not have become the unassuming, kind, and generous fellow he was if he had not grown, through his training in karate-do, to be ego-free.

Those lessons seemed long ago on that October afternoon when Lana stopped by the football field to pick Jeremy up. She was startled to see him inch his way toward the car as slowly as a caterpillar, supported by his six-foot, two-inch friend, Erik Yeager. Karate had taught Jeremy how to handle pain—not to try to fend it off but to move into it and go beyond it—so his face was peaceful, but it was clear to Lana that pain was there, and in no small amount. A slender shaft of fear danced like heat lightning around her heart and turned the tips of her fingers cold. She dismissed it as a hen's anxiety for her chick and even later could not persuade herself that in this moment she had had a presentiment that all of life was about to change.

She scrambled out of the car to meet Jeremy and was glad when he unhesitatingly threw his free arm around her neck and let her carry his weight along with Erik. "What happened, Jer? You must have hit the ground really hard."

"Like slamming off a mogul on a dirt bike," Yeager answered for him.

"What do you think, should I take you to the emergency room?"

"I just need to lie down," Jeremy said. A small sound, a bleat of pain, escaped him as he lowered himself to the car seat, but still he resisted Lana's impulse to take him to the hospital and assured Yeager that he would see him at school the next day. At home, using the banister to pull himself up the stairs, Jeremy groaned again as he had done getting into the car. "Man, this isn't funny," he admitted. "It really, really hurts."

By next morning the pain, which should have lessened with a night's rest and icing with cold packs, had if anything grown more intense. There was no question of Jeremy's going to school, but Lana was unsure what the next move should be. Jeremy was still insisting that he did not need to be seen by a doctor, but she suspected that was because of the expense. She longed for Roger to be there to help her decide what to do, but he was away for a month, in training for a new job as a safety inspector for the state of Oregon. By late afternoon, when she came back from teaching at the dojo and found that Jeremy was no better, she made the decision. "Come on, Jer," she said, "I'm taking you to the clinic. No arguments."

"Not from me," he said through teeth clamped against crying out.

The doctor on duty at the group practice clinic referred them to another facility for X rays, and by the time Lana had driven Jeremy there, he was unable to walk. She commandeered a wheelchair and eased him into it. Technicians lifted him onto the X-ray table, and the films confirmed what she had begun to suspect: Jeremy's pelvis was broken; there were multiple fractures.

"Rest," the doctor prescribed. "Minimal moving around, and you'll have to use crutches to keep your weight off the left side where the breaks are."

"Are you sure he shouldn't be in the hospital?" Lana asked. "I know my son and he's in an awful lot of pain."

Accustomed to children screaming over even minor hurts, the doctor was misled by Jeremy's composure. "He can rest just as well at home. I'll give him medication for the pain, and he should be better in a few days."

Still Lana hesitated.

"Mom's afraid she'll have to wait on me," Jeremy teased, his wide grin flashing.

"You'll owe me if I have to give you breakfast in bed every morning," she teased back, and capitulated, wheeling Jeremy to the car and adding her strength to his to lift him into the front seat.

Jeremy was no better a week later. Expense or not, Lana decided he had to be seen by an orthopedic surgeon. The specialist confirmed the diagnosis and told them the same thing: There were no measures to be taken except rest. Through the end of October, through November, and on into December, they were given the mantric response, "It takes time," whenever they returned to seek an answer as to why Jeremy's pain was not easing up, indeed almost seemed to be worsening. "It's like when a windshield gets smashed," the doctor told them. "For a time the cracks keep spreading." Lana found this a less than convincing explanation—that a shattered bone was not mending but fracturing further—but reluctantly she accepted it.

Jeremy tried to keep current with his schoolwork, played video games with his younger sister, Christen—Susanne, nineteen and married, had recently moved to Seattle—and entertained the friends who stopped by after school hours. His football-playing buddies came if practice ended while it was still light, but it was another Eric, Eric Lund, a friend made years before in church, who spent the most time with him. One late afternoon, when Lana got home from work, they suggested she might like to make them chocolate chip cookies but she declined, saying she was tired and needed a rest before starting dinner.

"Come on, Jer, we'll make them ourselves," said Eric. "It's easy." And so it was, and easier still for the two boys to polish them off, hot from the oven; and this became something for the two of them to do together almost every day.

Through the weeks, through good and bad days, Jeremy remained true to the code that martial artists greet fate with a bow, not a whine. Lana was proud of him, but still it baffled her why, with all Jeremy's patience, his youthful strength, and his history of body-building, improvement was so slow in coming. Several times when Roger was home on weekends, she asked what he thought they should do. Money was scarce, as it always was, but should she nevertheless take Jeremy to another specialist for a third opinion? Roger, with a male's impatience with illness, mostly shrugged and growled, "How should I know?" Sometimes he almost seemed angry, as though it were Jeremy's fault that he could no longer split logs for the stove that heated the house or ride with him on their dirt bikes in the woods. All the two still did together was watch car races on television, and they did that in silence.

Lana continued to procrastinate about a next move until Jeremy struggled into the house one wintry December afternoon after an attempt to shovel new-fallen snow off the front walk. "Mom, I think you better take me to the hospital. Something's really wrong." She wheeled to look at him. Jeremy's intensely blue eyes seemed drained of color, to be almost white. Now, finally, Lana did not hesitate. Minutes later they were in the car and driving to the Klamath Falls hospital.

They waited together in the emergency room after X rays had been taken, Jeremy lying like a wounded mountain cat in a curtained cubicle, still observant and powerful but helpless now, his jaw clenched, his hands in tight fists. Lana had once worked in this same hospital, in charge of arranging for lectures and educational films, so she knew most of the staff, including the doctor on duty in the emergency room this particular evening. The minute the technician emerged with Jeremy's X rays and slapped them up on the light box, Lana slipped from the cubicle and stood behind him and the doctor while they looked at them.

After long, long study and a look exchanged with the technician, the doctor cleared his throat.

And cleared it again.

Lana could stand the silence no longer. "What is it, Dr. Kesey? What are you seeing?"

"Look," the doctor said in a voice she had to bend forward to hear. He pointed to the X ray. "The left side of Jeremy's pelvis seems to have . . . disappeared . . . dissolved . . . been"—reluctantly he brought out the words—"eaten away."

Unbidden, unthought words leaped from Lana's mouth. "It's cancer, isn't it?" she whispered. Instantly she said firmly, "It's not cancer, is it?"

She hated the pity in Dr. Kesey's eyes when he turned. "I imagine the surgeons will want to do a biopsy to see what's going on."

Two years before, Lana had been with a friend when the friend's son was diagnosed with brain cancer, and her thought then had been, Oh, my God, what would I do if one of *my* children had cancer? Now she sucked in her breath, and when it became a sob, choked it off. She knew the answer. She would do the same thing her friend had done because it is the only thing you *can* do: You go on, you go forward, you do whatever has to be done. She said to Dr. Kesey, "Will you help me tell Jeremy?"

"How much do you want him to know?"

She stared at the X ray, at the baseball-sized shadow where there should have been strong white bone. "Jeremy lives in this body," she said—this heretofore impeccable body he so delightedly exercised, which performed with ease every task he set it. "He has a right to know. Tell him," she said, "what you've told me."

They could not have done anything else in any event because the minute Jeremy saw them he understood. His pain-clouded eyes cleared, and his gaze, suddenly focused, shot from his mother to the doctor and back.

"It looks like more than a break, Jeremy." The doctor took the boy's hand in his clasp. "It looks like it might be a tumor."

Lana did not understand why Jeremy let out his breath in a relieved sigh. "It might be serious, Jer," she said carefully.

"I know, Mom. But at least now something can be done about it. It's been really hard to hang around feeling so lousy and not know why."

Lana realized then the extent to which her son had been disciplining himself. She wanted to scold; she wanted to yell at him that sometimes it is better to demand attention, sometimes it does not make sense to be stoic, but she could not take his victory over pain away from him. She leaned down and kissed his forehead.

"We'll have to go in and take a look at it," the doctor said.

Jeremy asked, "What does that mean?"

"An operation. A biopsy. We need samples of tissue that can be examined under the microscope to tell us what we're dealing with."

"I've never had an operation," Jeremy said. "Heck, I've never even been sick if you don't count flu and chicken pox."

"It's all right to be scared," Lana told him fiercely.

"Of course, it is," the doctor backed her up. "But you'll be under anesthesia. You won't feel anything."

Jeremy was taken to the operating room the next morning. Roger and Christen waited with Lana. Members of what Lana thought of as her church family—the minister and two of her friends, Debbie Rappe and Martha Freeman—were also there. The children's biological father, Ron Schmaling, arrived from Sacramento. The atmosphere was prayerful as they waited for news. Lana did not offer promises to God because she did not believe that God made bargains, but in her heart she begged, *Please, God, please don't let Jeremy have cancer. Please cover my child with your peace and love. Please help us to deal with whatever lies ahead.*

Lana had only to look into the surgeon's weary eyes as he entered the waiting room to know the rockiness, the steepness, of the road ahead. "I'm afraid I can't give you good news," the surgeon said. "Jeremy's tumor looks malignant. It looks like bone cancer—perhaps Ewing's sarcoma, but we aren't certain."

Lana ran. She found herself in another part of the hospital, in Carol Hardin's office. Carol had also been a friend of the woman whose son died of brain cancer, and now the nightmare was starting for Jeremy and Lana. Carol pressed Lana's head into her shoulder and rocked her gently, her soft warm voice saying over and over, "Oh, Lana, Lana honey, Lana, Lana." Lana sobbed and Carol cried with her as two years before they had held their friend tight and grieved for her and her son.

Deep in the dark core where unacceptable knowledge is dumped, Lana knew that the diagnosis could signal the end of Jeremy's life. But she shoveled hope and resolve on top of that knowledge, and when she could dam her tears, she hurried back to the waiting room, determined to collect all possible information in order to deal with Jeremy's illness as intelligently as possible. But there was little the surgeon could tell her beyond the fact that immediately after Christmas, they would send Jeremy to Portland, to Doernbecher Hospital, a division of the University of Portland Hospital that specialized in the treatment of cancer in children. It was now December 22. Jeremy's condition was stable, the surgeon said, but they would keep him in the hospital for the time being because they had "a concern." The next day she learned what that concern was. Jeremy's tumor was heavily vascularized, laced by a network of blood vessels, and during surgery a large vessel had been nicked and it had been all but impossible to stop the bleeding.

"The blood just kept welling up," one of the doctors told her. "I had to put my thumb in the hole to try to stop it. We were afraid we'd lose him then and there."

Instead of later? Lana thought. And again she buried the thought under layers of resolve and hope.

"We've packed the incision with gauze," the doctor went on, "and are hoping that stops the oozing, but we'll have to watch him carefully through the next days to be sure he's out of the woods."

In the evening, when Jeremy was clear of the effects of the anesthesia, the surgeon threaded his way through Roger and Lana and Christen and stood at the foot of Jeremy's bed. It was Jeremy who spoke first. "Well, doc, what did you find out?"

"Jeremy, you have cancer and it is affecting the bones of your pelvis." The doctor's voice was low but steady and matter-of-fact.

"We'll be sending you to Portland for more tests to find out what kind of cancer it is and how best to deal with it."

Jeremy did not cry or turn his face away, but he began to shake as though with chill. "Mom, come here," he said. "Hold my hand." Lana would by choice have pulled him to her and cradled him in her arms, but not for anything would she destroy the dignity her son was struggling to preserve. Jeremy spoke to the doctor. "What can you do about the pain, sir? It is pretty uncomfortable."

"We'll give you medication for it."

"Thank you." He thought a moment. "Will I be able to go home for Christmas?"

"I don't see why not."

Jeremy nodded, and nodded again almost as though he were dismissing the surgeon, who also knew there was nothing more to say and turned and left the room. The silence was terrible. Lana buried her face in the pillow beside Jeremy and pulled his head hard against her cheek.

"It's going to be okay, Mom," Jeremy whispered. "Don't cry. I'll be okay." He was patting his mother's back as though he were the adult and she the child. "Take her home, Roger," he said to his stepfather. "I need to get some sleep."

How do you leave your fifteen-year-old son, Lana wondered in her heart, leave him in possession of news as frightening as any he will ever hear, leave the boy who has been courageous enough not to ask the doctor for hope, leave him alone with a burden of mortality that is not in your power to share? Roger nodded to her and led Christen from the room. Lana kissed Jeremy's forehead. "Okay, sweetie, I'll see you in the morning."

Stumbling down the corridor, she felt her arm caught by a man walking in the opposite direction. "Lana, what's wrong?" The man was Dave Chabner, a microbiologist at the hospital. "What's wrong?" he repeated as Lana stared at him dazedly.

"It's Jeremy. He has cancer. Oh, Dave!" He pulled her close and held her hard against the renewed sobs attacking her. "Oh, Dave, I don't know what to do."

He guided her into a small room and sat beside her, holding her hands. "Let's pray," he said, surprising her; she had not known scientists prayed. "Dear God," Dave began, without waiting for Lana to answer. He prayed aloud. Sometimes she heard the words; sometimes it was just the sound of his voice coming through the darkness that steadied her. "Remember, Lana," he said when they parted, "remember there is somewhere else to go when the going here gets too tough."

She did not see Dave again until Christmas Day, when he appeared in the doorway of Jeremy's room and asked if he might come in for a moment. Because Jeremy was still in pain, so much so that he had not repeated his request to go home for Christmas, Lana started to wave Dave away, but Jeremy smiled and Dave came forward.

"Would you mind if I prayed with you?" he asked Jeremy. Unself-consciously he dropped to his knees beside Jeremy's bed and asked God to make it possible for Jeremy to go home for Christmas. "Dear Lord, ease Jeremy's pain so he can go home in comfort," were his last words before he slipped out of the room again. How did he know about Jeremy's pain and his wish? He had read about the pain in Jeremy's chart, Lana decided, and, of course, any child wants to be home for Christmas; he could have guessed that.

Moments later Jeremy asked her to call the surgeon. "I'm ready to go home now," he said.

At home, Jeremy lay on the couch in the living room while he and Christen, Lana, and Roger took turns opening their presents. Christen borrowed Roger's pocketknife to slit the tape on a carton, the knife slipped, and blood surged from a gash in her knee so deep that Roger and Lana were quickly back in the hospital, waiting while the wound was stitched up in the emergency room. "Between you two kids, our family is falling apart," they joked with Christen. "We've got to start getting our act together."

The opening of Christmas presents, resumed when they arrived back at the house, was almost at an end when the color drained from Jeremy's face and he asked Roger to give him a hand climbing the stairs so he could get into bed. Christen stayed with

Lana, helping to clean up the scattered wrappings and arrange the open presents under the tree; then she too went up to bed. Roger led the way into the kitchen and sat Lana at the kitchen table while he built a fresh pot of coffee. There were plans to be made, things to be decided, money problems to be discussed, but Lana was content for the moment to be silent and feel Roger's touch on her shoulder as he walked back and forth between the cupboard and stove.

Christen burst through the door. "Mom, something's wrong with Jeremy! He's awful hot!"

Minutes later Lana was on the phone to the hospital to report that Jeremy was burning with fever. "Pack a bag," she was told. "We'll send an ambulance for you. You'll have to take him to Portland tonight."

Lana threw clothes into a carryall, all the time wanting to scream at Christen to be quiet so she could think, equally wishing she had time to comfort her because she knew how close Christen and Jeremy were and how frightened the girl was for her brother. Lana had never been able to provide much in the way of worldly goods for the children, but she had been able to keep them secure in the knowledge that they were unreservedly loved, and they had drawn on that well of love to care for and cherish each other.

Lights flashing, siren screaming, the ambulance sped Lana and Jeremy first to the hospital, where doctors hurriedly checked Jeremy's condition and administered morphine, then on to the airport where a Cessna "Lifeflight" plane was warming up to lift them over the mountains to Portland. The night was piercingly cold and a sleeting rain of ice and snow streamed over the plane's wings, but they could not wait for better weather. The plane shuddered down the runway and roared into the air. Lana was alone with Jeremy in the cabin; no doctor or nurse accompanied them. The pilot was at the controls, fighting the storm, somewhere in the darkness up ahead.

Jeremy, slamming his head from side to side in agony, clutched at Lana. "Mom, make this pain go away," he moaned. "I can't stand it. I can't stand it. I can't stand it!"

Helpless and terrified, her son in unendurable pain in the blackness of the night, perhaps dying, Lana closed her eyes, lifted her face, and prayed. "God, please help us," she pleaded. "God, please, please help us. *Please. Please.*" A feeling like warm water bathed the top of her head, flowed down, down into her neck, into her shoulders, down into her arms, down into the hands that Jeremy was gripping. His hands, squeezing hers until it seemed the small bones must crack, slowly loosened. Was he dead? Had he died? Lana opened her eyes. She looked at Jeremy. He was asleep. Peacefully asleep. A voice spoke quietly in the cabin. *"Don't be afraid, Lana. Jeremy will be cared for. Your son will be cared for."* Now she, too, was at peace. The strangling fear knotting her muscles and squeezing her heart melted like summer snow, and she sank back, resting as lightly as though she were cushioned in the clouds they were flying through.

In Portland, another screaming ambulance ride under flashing lights gave way to a dash through dim, empty, featureless hospital corridors. Awake now for twenty-four hours, as Lana ran behind the gurney carrying Jeremy, she sank into a dream state in which she seemed to be running in place, running forever in glacier fields while white-clad figures raced off with her son and she, on leaden legs, fell farther and farther behind.

The gurney disappeared and more white-jacketed figures materialized from every direction, converging on a room in which there was no place for Lana. She braced her back against a wall in the corridor and listened to her pounding heart. This was the hospital in Portland, she told herself. They had made it this far. The people in there were doctors; they were fighting to keep her son alive. Would he survive the night? The hovering peace experienced during the flight was gone and she could not call it back. All that filled her now was emptiness and dread.

The flood of white coats reversed, surging out of the room. One doctor spoke as he passed, the words floating into the air above Lana's head. "The boy is stable. Tests tomorrow." She edged into the room. Jeremy's eyes were shut and his skin was as pale as though he had never experienced sunlight. What now? Stay? Go?

Stay, of course. Watch over Jeremy. Did they give him morphine? Will he sleep through the hours until morning? She sat beside his bed in a straight chair while an hour lurched by in the rustling anonymity of the hospital. Time and again her head slumping forward jerked her awake. If she fell off the chair, she might wake Jeremy, consigning him once more to the ferocious pit of pain. She decided to seek the nurses' station and ask if there was a vacant bed or a couch in a waiting room where she might lie down.

A man talking to the duty nurse paused politely to allow her to put her question, and it was he who answered. "I know a place where you can stay. It's the Ronald McDonald House and it's just a block away. I'll take you there."

Lana looked to the nurse. "This man is the manager of it," the nurse verified, and promised to call her if Jeremy woke up.

Four hours later Lana was back in the hospital, following the gurney through the corridors as Jeremy was taken for a CAT scan. He had to lie utterly still on a hard, flat, icy metal surface for forty-five minutes. While she watched, she saw his sky-blue eyes turn white, his face take on a colorless glow, and she knew he had traveled through his pain to the beyond.

His room was crowded when he was returned to it. Roger and Christen, having started in the darkness before dawn to drive the six hours through the storm to Portland, were there. Susanne, Jeremy's older sister, coming from Seattle, had stopped on the way and picked up her grandmother, Lana's mother. Their presence was comforting—Lana felt less devastatingly alone—but between the huge fears none of them dared to put into words and commonplace thoughts not worth expressing, they were mostly silent as they sat waiting for the doctors to bring them word—as they sat waiting for the fateful future to arrive.

2
A Special Dog

The doctor who laid out the immediate future was reassuringly middle-aged, his face responsibly lined, his hair thinning and steel-colored. Although Lana and Roger were both present at the meeting in his office, Dr. Nerhout addressed Jeremy, according him full status as the person to make the decisions, perhaps because he read in the set of Jeremy's head that the boy accepted the responsibility and believed it belonged to him. When Jeremy was a youngster, Lana assumed it was his flaxen hair and wide, engaging smile that drew people's eyes to him, but lately she had begun to think it was something more, an air of quiet, uninsistent self-possession.

Dr. Nerhout tented his fingers and looked over them. "Jeremy," he said in an even voice, "you have Ewing's sarcoma, which is a rare form of bone cancer. The cancer has metastasized to your lungs; that is, tumors are present in your lungs as well as in your pelvis. We have courses of treatment to try, but it will be a really hard, tough fight and we cannot tell what the odds are of your coming through it because each case is different." With the back of his index finger, the doctor eased his glasses off his nose and resettled them higher. "The pain we can help you with, but your cancer is in a bad spot. To fight it is going to be far more difficult than anything you've ever had to face, far, far more difficult. It is up to you to decide whether you want to make the fight."

Jeremy did not hesitate, did not look to Roger or his mother for their assent. "I'm ready," he said firmly. "Let's get started."

"You're sure?"

Dr. Nerhout was essentially giving Jeremy a choice between possibly living and certainly dying, and Lana thought it wholly strange that the doctor asked for confirmation of this Hobson's choice until the sad thought occurred to her that perhaps he wanted to be able to remind Jeremy later, when death might seem preferable, that he had had his chance to say no to the terrors of treatment.

"I'm sure."

The doctor nodded, accepting Jeremy's decision. "We have more tests to do," he said, standing up behind his desk. "After we have the results, we'll talk again."

When Dr. Nerhout next spoke to Jeremy, it was to warn him that the chemotherapy to be given would make him very, very ill because they intended to use the most aggressive treatment possible. Although sedative medication might lessen the misery somewhat, Jeremy would throw up repeatedly, his hair would fall out, and he would feel wretched beyond description. Again the doctor asked the boy, "Are you sure you want to go through this?" "I'm a fighter," Jeremy answered. "When you're ready, I am."

To Lana, in private, Dr. Nerhout said, "We have had a few survivors of Ewing's sarcoma, Mrs. Stewart, but if I'm to be honest with you, I have to warn you that Jeremy's chances are not good."

"I don't care about the odds," Lana told him. "I firmly believe, and always have, that when it's your time, nothing will help, but if it's not your time, a way will open up for you to survive. I don't know if my son is meant to live, but if he is, I'll do anything it takes to see him through."

"By the time treatment is over, you will know every tree, every rock, every turn in the road between Klamath Falls and Portland, you will have driven it so many times."

"If you told me I had to walk it or crawl it, I would still say yes," Lana replied. "Jeremy realizes, and I do too, that you cannot promise us anything but a cruel and difficult time. But that cruel time may be a crack Jeremy can slip through to get back into the ordinary world. We'll try for that chance no matter what."

"Right," the doctor said. "Right," he repeated as he rose to see her out of his office. "You have a determined son, and acorns don't fall far from the tree, do they? We will do what we can, Mrs. Stewart, everything we can."

There was a necessary lull before the chemotherapy storm while intensive antibiotic treatment was administered to eradicate the infection in the eight-inch-long biopsy incision in Jeremy's groin. The doctors explained that the infection had to be dealt with first because chemotherapy would seriously weaken his immune system, allowing the infection to come surging back if it was still lurking. Lana, alone now that Roger and Christen had returned to Klamath Falls and Susanne and Lana's mother to Seattle, spent the days and some or all of the nights with Jeremy at the hospital. On fine days she slipped out to take a half-hour run in the afternoon to drain away some of the worry and tension. Jeremy could not go with her, of course, as he had often done at home, sometimes running teasing circles around her on their five-mile conditioning runs, but he did shoulder and arm exercises sitting in bed to keep from losing strength through inaction. After ten days, the doctors pronounced his infection cleared and the chemotherapy "hookup" was scheduled for the following morning.

Lana walked to the hospital in the first light of day while civilization's sins against nature were still hidden in the dawn and the skies were fresh, the air clean. She found Jeremy sitting on the edge of his bed and a nurse readying an injection of Ativan, a sedative that would put him in a semiconscious state to help him endure the effects of the chemotherapy. "Here, I'll pop a vein for you," Jeremy said to the nurse, and clenched his fist, tightening his muscles until a pulsating vein obligingly tented his skin on the inside of his elbow.

"Hey, that's a neat trick," the nurse applauded. "Wish you could teach it to the other kids."

"It would be in vain," Jeremy said, and grinned as the young nurse made a face at his pun.

When he popped a vein for her again, it was for the hookup proper, the first of three bags of chemicals to be given in succession over a period of about three hours. He and Lana stared at the plastic tube as the mesmerizing drops began to slide down the line—*drip . . . drip . . . drip . . . drip . . . drip*—the killing chemicals joining the blood streaming through his vascular tree to split off—where? . . . how? How discriminating were the chemicals? Did they bypass good cells to chew up the bad or swarm over everything in their path? Like industrial toxins spilt in a river, did the poisons turn the flow green and sluggish? The images kept coming in Lana's mind until Jeremy began to vomit. He vomited . . . and vomited . . . and vomited, seventy-five times, a hundred times, rolling over on his side just enough to retch into the basin she held jammed against his cheek. Occasionally he murmured, "That's rad" or "That's gross" or "Did it again, Mom," trying to joke a little as she wiped his face with a damp washcloth.

Lana did not dare leave him unless a nurse was with him, and now she understood the drained, exhausted-looking women she encountered in the halls. They constituted a desperately frightened sorority of mothers standing guard over the fragile bodies of their children to see that they did not choke on their own vomit, to summon immediate help if a needle worked loose or an IV line fell away, to hold basins and bring bedpans, to offer water and bathe faces with cooling cloths. All the time, Lana knew from snatches of talk, they wondered and worried about their other children at home. Was the children's father holding the family together, seeing to meals and clean clothes, that homework got done and chores were not neglected, that the rituals of the family, like tucking into bed and reading stories and good-night kisses, were being continued? Or were the children running wild, building up resentment over the attention and concern concentrated on one child, perhaps suffering guilt over their own good health, perhaps skirting or sliding into depression over the fate of a sibling? Was their father attentive, supportive, sensitive to their needs? Or—the unworthy but unbanishable thought—were his own needs and fears driving him outside the family, outside the home, to seek solace for himself?

As she exchanged bare, revealing sentences over the washbasins in the ladies' room or shared a table for a quick cup of coffee in the cafeteria with the drawn women battling to keep the flame of a child's life from flickering out, Lana learned that the fracture lines in the families of several of the women were already so severe as to be beyond mending. The wives felt bitterly alone in their terrible vigil, while the husbands felt cheated of the channel through which their emotions customarily flowed. Resentments grew; arguments flared; silences became unbridgeable. Lana wondered if she was destined to join this contingent of wives who, while perhaps losing a child, had already lost a husband? She could not be absolutely confident that it would not happen. Roger and she had a passionate marriage, each of them supremely content in the physical presence of the other, each of them, schooled by karate, in tune with their bodies and accustomed in their minds to think in terms of courage and responsibility. But Roger felled giant trees and rode motorcycles; he was a doer, a man whose outlets were robust. It was Lana who was the sink and the source—the sink for troubles to wash into, the source for renewal as fresh and clear as water from a spring. Could Roger endure a role reversal? Could he let Lana pour herself into Jeremy and come to him, Roger, for renewal, or would he, like fully half the husbands of the hollow-eyed women on this floor of children with cancer, need to find his own replenishment in someone else? Only time would answer the question of Roger, as only time could answer the question of Jeremy.

When that first bout of chemotherapy was over, it was the end of January and Lana took Jeremy home to Klamath Falls. His schedule of treatment from now on was set at one week in the hospital followed by three weeks at home to give him time to regain as much of his strength as possible. But after they had been home that first time for just two days, again came the sudden onset of fever, again the ambulance screaming in the night, again the flight to Portland. Back in the hospital the doctors discovered a huge abscess in Jeremy's groin at the biopsy site. The infection had raged back from supposed extinction. The abscess had to be cleaned out surgically.

"Oh, Mom, I don't think I can get through this." Exhausted from the bout of chemotherapy, ill, fever-ridden, Jeremy's resolve had drained away, and he clung to her. "I'm afraid. I'm so afraid."

Lana held him and rocked him. "Sweetie, I don't know how to help you. The doctors here are experts. We've got to trust that they know the right things to do and that somehow things will work out." The meager words were little comfort to Jeremy, but she could think of nothing else to say. He fell back against the pillow. She gripped his hand, and they were silent.

Late that evening, long after visiting hours were over, a knock came on the partially open door of the room and a white-haired, blue-eyed, benign-looking gentleman peered around it. "Jeremy? We've come to see you. Is that okay?" He was followed into the room by another gentleman, equally elderly, equally dignified in a business suit, and quite as distinguished-looking. The first man moved to the foot of Jeremy's bed and rested his hands lightly on the railing. "Jeremy," he said in a voice comfortingly pitched between lightness and gravity, "I have a message for you from God. If you don't mind, I'd like to share it with you."

Jeremy, rather than looking startled, leaned back against his pillows and the fear seeped from his face as he opened thirstily to the peace radiated by the man at the foot of his bed. Lana drifted back as the other man moved into her place at Jeremy's side. She felt her own arms drop to her sides, and her whole being—her breathing, her heartbeat—seemed to go into suspension, as though she were in shock, but it was a serene, cotton-batting type of shock, devoid of concern for Jeremy, for herself, for what was happening.

The man opened the Bible he carried and began to read, inserting Jeremy's name in the scripture:

Jeremy, you will dwell in the shelter of the Most High,
will rest in the shadow of the Almighty,
You will say of the Lord, "He is my refuge and my fortress;
my God, in whom I trust."
Jeremy, He will save you from the fowler's snare
and from the deadly pestilence;
He will cover you with his feathers,
and under his wings you will find refuge;
His faithfulness will be your shield and rampart.
Jeremy, you will not fear the terror of the night,
nor the arrow that flies by day,
nor the pestilence that stalks in darkness,
nor the plague that destroys at midday.

and on to the end:

Jeremy, because the Lord loves you, He will rescue you;
He will protect you for He acknowledges your name,
Jeremy Christopher Schmaling.
He will call upon you, and you will answer Him;
He will be with you in trouble,
He will deliver you and honor you.
With long life will He satisfy you,
and show you your salvation.

From far off, Lana heard the man say, "Do you have your Bible here, Jeremy?" And when Jeremy said that he did, the man said, "Look up Psalm Ninety-one and read it when you need comfort. The Lord loves you, Jeremy. May God bless you."

Then the men were gone. The room was empty. Lana and her son looked at each other wordlessly, until Jeremy whispered, "Wow, am I glad they came!"

The men, one silent, one the conveyor of a message, had comforted her son in a way Lana had not been able to. She hurried out of the room to thank them. The halls were bathed in the hush and long blue emptiness of hospital corridors at night. "Which way did they go?" she asked the nurse at the station directly opposite Jeremy's door.

The nurse glanced up amiably. "Which way did who go?"

"The ministers, the chaplains, whoever they were, the two men who were just here."

"Nobody's been here. The chaplain doesn't come unless we call him."

"Well, the Seventh-Day Adventists or whatever, the two men in business suits. They were just here. You couldn't *not* have seen them."

"No one's been on the floor tonight." The nurse was willing to be helpful but was puzzled and shook her head.

Lana turned away, then turned back. "What does the chaplain look like?"

"He's short, balding."

The men visiting Jeremy had been tall with trimmed silvery hair. Lana briefly wondered if she should be angry that the floor nurse was so absorbed in her charts that she paid no attention to who came and went on the floor. Should she report the nurse to her supervisor? It was dangerous to have unaccounted-for strangers drifting into the rooms of sick children. Or was it? Those strangers had brought Jeremy peace, taken away his fear. She went back in the room and saw that Jeremy was deep in easeful sleep.

A few days after the operation, when he had regained some strength, Jeremy asked his mother to wheel him to the bathroom down the hall. He longed to have a proper bath but was not allowed to get in the tub by himself and could not bear for one of the young nurses to be witness to his nakedness. Lana ran the water, steadied Jeremy as he stepped into the tub, scrubbed his back, and at his suggestion began to shampoo his hair.

"What's the matter?" he asked when her hands faltered. "Mom, are you crying?"

"No, no . . ." She tried to rub her eyes against her sleeve.

"Is it my hair? Is it starting to come out?"

"It means the chemicals are working." Lana's hands were covered, matted, with his golden hair. For the first time in front of him, she broke down and sobbed. "Oh, Jer—"

"They said it would fall out."

"Yes, and it doesn't matter," she insisted. "It doesn't matter." But it did. It was a small death, a foretaste, a dress rehearsal. Suddenly she wanted the hair off her hands. She was in a panic to get it off. She scrubbed her hands on a towel, rubbing, rubbing until the hair was all over the floor. Then she was down on her knees trying to gather it up.

"Mom. . . ."

"I'll get some more towels." She left him then, long enough to stop trembling, and when she came back, his head had only stubble on it. He had rubbed off all the hair that would come off.

"You'll have to give me a buzz cut, Mom. I'll look like Michael Jordan."

"You'll be at least as handsome as Yul Brynner."

"Whoever he is."

"A movie star. You're too young to remember."

"Hand me one of those towels. I'll make a Turk's turban."

They were making light of it, but a line had been crossed. Now Jeremy belonged not to the ordinary world but to the killing fields of cancer.

Seven days, eight days, sometimes it was ten days before Jeremy recovered enough strength after the bout with chemotherapy for the six-hour drive back home to Klamath Falls. It was during one of those periods at home, in March, that Lana took Jeremy to visit Ella Brown and Ella loaned Jeremy the book about German shepherds.

Jeremy had difficulty reading because the treatment affected his eyes, but he would not give up on the book. He made his way steadily and thoughtfully through each page, however long it took, and absorbed everything the book had to tell him before returning it, in perfect condition, to Ella.

On another trip back home two months later, the telephone was ringing as Jeremy made his way into the house on his crutches. Lana answered it. On the line was the principal of the junior high school, the Henley School, which Jeremy had attended before moving on to the senior high the previous fall. The students, the principal told Lana, had been selling candy and apples all term, raising money for Jeremy, and what they wanted most of all was for Jeremy to come to the school so they could present their gift and the cards they had made to him in person.

Lana relayed the message to Jeremy. "Mom, I can't do it," he said quickly. "I can't face the kids."

"They'll be disappointed."

"I've been through enough."

Lana knew what he had been through: the endless days and nights in the hospital, the procedures, the needles, the trailing tubes, the emesis basins, the loss of strength, the indignities of illness. She knew, too, what he was thinking: when the students had last seen him, he had been a strong, straight-backed, golden, graceful lad with everything going for him, and now he was a tired, thin, sick boy on crutches with no hair and an uncertain future.

She brought him a cup of hot soup and pulled up a chair beside the couch. "What are you afraid of, Jer?"

"You know, Mom."

"Yes." She thought for a while. "Tell me this. What would you think of a boy who had no hair because he had to go through chemotherapy to save his life?"

"I'd tell him he was crazy if he thought it mattered."

"Yes," she said again, and waited.

"Okay, Mom, call the school. Tell them I'll come."

At midmorning the next day, the students were watching for Jeremy, and when Lana swung the car into the school drive, the big double doors of the school burst open and teenagers streamed out, running to the car and surrounding it. Husky football players lifted Jeremy and carried him into the school's gymnasium. Two hundred kids, boys he had known all his life, played with, biked with, practiced karate with, girls he had teased, danced with, ridden the school bus with, crowded around him, shaking his hand, hugging him, saying, "Oh, Jeremy, we're so glad to see you!" Then he was picked up again, this time to be set down midway up the bleachers while the kids filled the rows in a great circle around him. Their caring warmed the air as they asked how he was doing, how it was for him, and vied in telling him tales out of school.

"Okay, Jer," one fellow said, indicating the scarf tied pirate fashion around Jeremy's head, "it's time to take it off."

"No!" Jeremy reached protectively to his head.

A girl said, "You need to do this, Jeremy. You need to know that we love you anyway, that it doesn't matter about your hair."

A guy agreed, "We're with you, Jer."

After a moment Jeremy let his hand drop away, and someone behind him tugged gently at the scarf. It slid off. A girl leaned down and kissed his bare, shining head. A boy followed suit, and another and another, boys and girls alike. "We love you. We're here for you, Jer. Don't forget that."

"Thanks, you guys, it means a lot to me."

A boy handed him an envelope. "We want you to have this, Jer. We're praying for you." Inside was three hundred dollars.

The bell rang, signifying the end of a class period. The principal's voice came over the intercom. "Time's up, kids. We agreed you'd have one class off and that's it." But no one moved, and the five or six teachers who were lined up against the wall made no gesture. Twice more the bell rang for the end of a period, but not until Jeremy said, "I think I need to go now, guys," did the kids line up to hug him for a last time and file out.

As Lana drove him home, Jeremy several times marveled: "That's such a lot of money for the kids to have raised. It's such a lot." Most of the families were like theirs—living close to the line, just making it—and Jeremy well knew that three hundred dollars for these kids was like three thousand or even thirty thousand for kids in other parts of the country, other walks of life.

That afternoon another call came, this time from the principal at the regional high school Jeremy had attended for only a month in the fall. Would Jeremy come to an assembly at the senior high? The students there had also been raising money and wanted to present it to him.

When Lana delivered Jeremy at the high school the next morning, the doors were open and inside were row upon row upon row of students, a thousand teenagers packing the gymnasium, with the school band playing. The football team escorted Jeremy to the middle of the gymnasium floor, and there Jeremy stood, braced on his crutches, tears in his eyes, while the crowd gave him a standing ovation. Jeremy kept saying, "Thanks, you guys," but the applause went on and on, until finally a member of the football team stepped up beside Jeremy and signaled for quiet. The principal handed Jeremy a microphone and asked him to say a few words, and with the local news media there filming him, Jeremy looked around at the sea of faces and began to speak.

"I want to thank all of you for supporting me in this fight. During the lonely nights in the hospital, I'd look at your cards stuck up all over the walls of my room and I'd feel better because I knew so many of you cared. All I can say to you in return is: Think positive. Make each day count. There is nothing in life you can't overcome if you have faith. Keep up the spirit. We are going to win."

The crowd was on its feet again, cheering. The band struck up the football fight song, and one of the cheerleaders came forward to present Jeremy with a check and more stacks of homemade cards. The principal took the microphone to announce that any student who wished to visit Jeremy at home at any time had only to come to the principal's office and ask for a pass to be excused from classes.

Lana thought a lot about those two school visits, whether Jeremy was special or whether it would have been the same for any kid with cancer, and she decided that both interpretations were true. Jeremy was special because he had often been in the newspapers as the fair-haired athlete, because everyone knew him, because he had always been popular; but there would also have been an outpouring for any kid with cancer because of something unbearably poignant about this threat to a young life. The kids identified because it might be them; parents identified because it might be their child.

Jeremy's friends did not abuse the privilege of asking to be excused from classes to visit him, well knowing that Jeremy's strength was slow to rebuild following the chemotherapy bouts in Portland, but often one or two or three would drop by in the afternoon. If Jeremy felt too exhausted and ill to get out of bed, they joined him in his bedroom, but on good days Erik Yeager, whom everyone called Big Bubba, gathered him up and carried him downstairs to take him for a ride. Then Lana would know it was all right to duck out on errands or go for a run. It was not that she was so fond of running but she needed the runs to put her in a different space for a while, a space apart from fear and tension.

It happened that on one afternoon when Jeremy was downstairs and lying on the couch, Ella Brown called. "I wonder if you and Jeremy could come out here?" she asked Lana. That was all she said, but Jeremy readily agreed to the drive, and when they pulled up outside the kennel, Ella was waiting. She opened a gate and the eight German shepherd puppies Lana and Jeremy had seen in March barged out, no longer fur balls but all loose legs and big ears and exuberance. Except for one. Ella said, "I want you to meet a special dog," and as though he had understood her, the one quiet puppy walked over to Jeremy and woofled, deep in his throat, low and meditative, as he sniffed Jeremy's hand. Jeremy leaned down and the dog snuffled his cheek and neck in an exploratory dog kiss that was a model of dignified restraint.

"What a handsome, *handsome* puppy," said Jeremy. "But why is he whimpering, Ella? Doesn't he like me?"

"He's not whimpering, Jeremy," Ella said. "He's talking. That's his way of talking to you. Once in a great while there will be a dog in a litter, a special dog, who is a talker."

"Oh." Jeremy bent over again. "Hello, pup," he told the dog seriously. "If you're saying you like me, I like you, too."

"He's a special dog," Ella repeated. "He's Rainy Ridge's son, and Rainy was a grand champion. This dog is going to look a lot like him when he's grown, I think."

"And be as intelligent," Jeremy added. "You can see it in his eyes."

Ella seemed to be studying the dog and did not look at Jeremy as she said, "I have a notion this dog'd be best off belonging to a special boy, and I wondered if you might want to have him."

Happiness blazed in Jeremy's face—and abruptly died away. "Ella, thank you, but I know how valuable your puppies are," he said, "and we don't have any money."

Money, the lack of it, always more or less a concern for Lana and Roger, had by now swelled into a problem of nightmarish proportions. Roger had been hired by the state of Oregon just a month before Jeremy's cancer was discovered, and the health insurance provider was refusing to pay for Jeremy's treatment on the basis that his illness was a preexisting condition. Patty Garbutt, the wife of a lawyer in Klamath Falls and mother of a music student of Lana's, had established the Jeremy Schmaling fund, and contributions to it were helping to pay some of the bills, which were escalating rapidly and eventually were to total nearly a million dollars, but that fund was in the hands of trustees. None of the money came to the family, and they had to pay for the gas to get to Portland and back, food on the way, food and a room for Lana in Portland—the Ronald McDonald House was not free; it cost ten dollars a night and sometimes it was full, forcing her to stay in a motel. She needed to buy milkshakes, fried chicken, ice cream for Jeremy, whatever he thought he might be able to eat and sent her out on midnight runs to find for him. Their old car gave out and had to be replaced. Roger prowled the secondhand lots for the cheapest one he could find still in running condition, but a car, however cheap, costs money and Lana was not earning anything. She had had to give up her piano teaching, which had brought in several hundred dollars a month; and the karate studio, with neither Jeremy nor Lana there for the classes they customarily taught, was contributing little.

Ella was not surprised to hear that money was a problem. "What I had in mind," she told Jeremy, "was not to sell him but for you and I to be partners in the puppy."

"Partners?"

"Co-owners. This dog needs to be in a home, not a kennel, and he needs a particular person who belongs to him that he can grow up with. If you could raise him, I could take care of his shots and vet bills and keep him here when you have to be in the hospital." She elaborated rather severely, as though it might be a sticking point, "It would have to be understood that when he is grown, as co-owner I'd share the breeding rights."

"Yes. Fine. Sure." Jeremy was stammering. "But if he's such a special dog . . . Ella, I'm afraid I might not be able to do a good job raising him."

"Like I told you, you treat a puppy like you'd treat a child. Talk to him. Explain what you expect of him— he'll understand. Praise him, encourage him. Tell him when he's being good and redirect him when he's not. Give him lots of reasons to feel good about himself and learn to trust himself. You can do that."

"Yes. Oh, Ella . . ." His voice broke and he leaned down to hide his face against the dog.

Ella checked with Lana. "Is it all right with you if Jeremy has the puppy?"

Lana was not thinking about what Ella had said about this being a special dog when she swiftly gave her consent, nor was she to realize until a long time later just how special he was. For the moment he was simply a puppy whose companionship her son badly needed, and she was silently blessing the generosity of this woman who would let a valuable animal go to the boy who needed him rather than to the person who had the money to pay for him.

Ella made out an impressively official bill of sale and a second document of co-ownership, which Jeremy signed with a prideful flourish. Jeremy then put it to Ella that since they were co-owners, they must be jointly responsible for naming the puppy. Ella agreed, and because she had been naming this line of dogs after mountains, she brought out an atlas for them to consult. It was

Jeremy who spotted a mountain in Alaska called Grizzly Ridge. He looked down at the puppy, who was lying at his feet. "Grizzly?" he said. The dog's head lifted alertly.

"Grizzly, come here," Ella said, holding out her hand. The puppy scrambled to his feet and went to her. "Yes," said Ella. "That fits. That's the right name for him."

Jeremy held the puppy snuggled in his lap as he and Lana headed home in the car. "Grizzly Ridge von Braun Schmaling," he whispered in the dog's ear. "My dog Griz." The car angled around a curve, and a second sharp curve, and the puppy threw up. Jeremy chortled delightedly, "You're my dog all right, Griz," he said. "You throw up just like me."

Grizzly's only other transgression came a month later when a roast momentarily left on the kitchen counter was gone when Roger came in from the living room to slice it. Dog and greasy traces of the meat were located in Jeremy's room. Lana suggested a spanking, Roger urged a beating, but Jeremy would not hear of it. After explaining clearly but unemphatically to Grizzly that it was wrong to steal, Jeremy guaranteed that it would not happen again, and it never did. Housebreaking the puppy was accomplished in the same fashion—by Jeremy telling Grizzly what he expected of him—and was successfully completed in a couple of days.

When Jeremy was able, the dog and the boy went outside together, Grizzly obedient to the conversational sound of Jeremy's voice and almost clairvoyantly attuned to his meaning. But if Jeremy felt too ill to walk with the dog, he just opened the front door. Grizzly would run around and around the house to give himself the exercise he needed and then hurry back inside and lie down near where Jeremy rested, on the couch or upstairs in his room.

That year, during the times Jeremy had to be in Portland, Grizzly stayed at Ella's and was in the charge of the five adult dogs, who were free to move around the property, from kennel to office to house, and free to approach any person, client or friend or tradesman, since they were perfectly mannered. Without fuss, they saw to it that Grizzly became so too, communicating with eye contact, lifted lip, low warning growls, and threatened nips when he stepped out of line. Grizzly liked being with his pack family, but he was always listening for Jeremy's whistle, Ella said, and when he heard it, he flew to Jeremy's side and never looked back. Sometimes Jeremy was too ill to fetch him. Then Ella drove him to the house and Grizzly hurried inside and up the stairs to Jeremy's room. When he felt Jeremy's hand on his head and heard Jeremy's voice answering the interrogative thrumming deep in his own throat, he subsided quietly on the braided rug beside the bed or, if Jeremy invited him, climbed carefully up on the bed to stretch his length beside Jeremy and lie there with Jeremy's arm around him.

He soon became so attuned to Jeremy that he was able to distinguish the times when Jeremy was physically too ill and worn to leave his bed and the times when it was discouragement that kept Jeremy housebound. When he sensed it was the latter, Grizzly snapped his teeth lightly and repeatedly to make a clacking sound. This amused Jeremy, and when he chuckled, Grizzly wagged his tail and chirked encouragingly to chivy Jeremy into rousing and going for a walk with him.

When they stopped to let Jeremy rest on those walks, Jeremy talked to his dog about life and luck, hope and death, his dreams and his reality. At least, that was Lana's guess because sometimes at night in the hospital she and Jeremy would talk and he seemed more and more at home with his deepest thoughts, as though he had already voiced them and grown familiar with them.

He said things like: "Mom, I used to listen to my friends talking about what they wanted to be when they grew up, and I'd wonder why I didn't see myself grown up. I'd try to picture myself and nothing would come. Do you suppose it's because I'm not going to get to be grown up?"

Grizzly could respond to such thoughts with woofling sounds, suiting his vocal riffs to the tone of Jeremy's voice and whatever he understood of Jeremy's meaning, which Lana suspected was an uncommon amount. She was not so lucky; she had to find words, or so she felt, until one day she realized that she too needed only sounds to have Jeremy know that her heart beat with his heart, that if there were answers, she did not have them, only, like Grizzly, immeasurable love for her boy.

Jeremy was the oldest child on the floor at Doernbecher, which meant that he was more acutely aware of the implications of his diagnosis than most of the other patients. The younger children, burdened with far less knowledge about the odds in cancer and the therapeutic tortures to come, for the most part accepted their illness and thought of what they could do rather than what they could not. They were fearful, of course, of needle pokes and painful procedures, particularly of bone-marrow biopsy since it entailed the forcing, without anesthetic, of a large needle through bone to reach and withdraw the marrow. Over and over they screamed, "Mommy! Mommy!" but when the procedure was over, they went quickly back to playing video games and riding tricycles in the halls.

Jeremy, being older and in touch with himself, took illness as a challenge—for growth, for learning, for living in the moment in the best way he could manage. He made friends with everyone, joked with the nurses and teased them, sat on the edge of the bed doing exercises to bulk up his biceps, and with his friend Eric Lund raced through the halls doing "wheelies," riding on the back tires of wheelchairs with the front ones in the air. Eric, two years older than Jeremy and his best friend, had promised Jeremy, when he learned of the cancer, "I will be there with you. I'll be there for you." His word cost him a good deal, but he had meant it and he kept it. Each Friday whenever Jeremy was in the hospital, Eric's mother met Eric at the high school with his overnight bag and drove him to the bus station in Klamath Falls. Another relative met him at the bus station in Portland and drove him to the hospital, and at two in the morning he would pop into Jeremy's room. "Okay, Mom," he'd whisper to Lana, "I'll take over now. Get some rest." And every Sunday night he'd make the return trip, arriving back in Klamath Falls in time to get to school Monday morning.

Late at night was the hardest time for Jeremy, especially when a hookup was scheduled for the next morning. He talked to Eric then about his fears, about God and faith, and together they prayed. But when daylight came, they were boys together, pinning a *Sports Illustrated* swimsuit picture at the head of Jeremy's bed to tease a young nurse who was nine months pregnant, bumming uneaten food off trays to keep Eric fed, working on Eric's homework together, watching ball games on television. Lana never hesitated to leave Jeremy with Eric. He was as tender as a woman when Jeremy needed bathroom help or nursing care or the emesis basin held against his cheek, and when Jeremy needed comforting, Eric unashamedly held his hand and rubbed his forehead. He and Jeremy were both blessedly free of gender identity hang-ups, two beautiful young men, manly, masculine, but truly loving each other.

By summer of that first year, treatment—the course of chemotherapy followed by six weeks of daily radiation—was complete and Jeremy was better, much better: "clear," the doctors said. Because he had worked at keeping himself in shape, at building muscle instead of acquiescing in the loss of it, with the cessation of the debilitating treatment, Jeremy quickly began to seem like his old self. His hair was coming back in and, to the doctors' amazement, his pelvic bone was regenerating, growing back strongly enough for him to walk without crutches, strongly enough for him to play football with Grizzly. "Go get it, Griz!" he'd shout and let loose a long pass, which Grizzly would jump to knock down. Getting a grip on the ball by sinking his teeth into the laces, the dog would run the ball back, dodging Jeremy the tackler. Jeremy had been warned that if he broke his pelvis again, his leg would have to be amputated, but the risk did not seem great to him and he played full out.

Jeremy had turned sixteen in March, which made him eligible for a driver's license, and in midsummer he applied for it. He and Roger located a little blue pickup that Jeremy got in exchange for a motorcycle, a chain saw, and fifty dollars. After he and Roger cleaned and tuned the motor, the pickup ran fine and Jeremy would take Grizzly for long, leisurely drives. Grizzly, sitting tall on the seat beside Jeremy with a seat belt strapped around his chest, watched the scenery with seeming interest and called Jeremy's attention to anything that caught his eye, like cows or horses or other dogs. "*M-m-m-m,*" he would say deep in his throat, and Jeremy would follow his glance and say, "You're right, Griz, it's a horse. Think you could outrun him?"

"*Um-m-m-m.*"

"Now you're bragging. But you're better looking, I'll give you that. You are one handsome dog, Griz."

At the end of the summer the Make-A-Wish Foundation underwrote a trip to Florida for the family, and when Jeremy asked, "Could I take my best buddy too?" they included Eric Lund, paying for meals, hotel, rental car, and gas, and even supplying money for extras. Jeremy wanted to see the Everglades and the Kennedy Space Center, but the Foundation had a package deal with Walt Disney World, so they went there first. The boys were too old to be intrigued by its fantasy but were fascinated by Epcot Center and, when they moved on to the coast, by the Space Center at Cape Canaveral. At Cocoa Beach, they rented surfboards, which Lana knew how to ride from her years of living in California. She instructed Jeremy and Roger—Eric, not a strong swimmer, stayed behind on the beach—in how to read the wave patterns, that they usually came in threes, with the third wave being the largest. Roger never quite caught a wave, but Jeremy was such a natural athlete that he was quickly up and skimming across the water, whooping with glee.

That and driving a brand-new convertible with the top down on the flat roads of Florida thrilled Jeremy. Indeed, they all loved the trip. It was a rollicking, high, hopeful time of new sights, laughter, and the joy of being a family again, a continent away from violent therapy and killing fields.

3
The Last Drive Home

That fall, everywhere Jeremy went, Grizzly walked or rode by his side. Jeremy usually had his hand resting lightly on Grizzly's head, perhaps less to guide Grizzly than to reassure himself, as though Grizzly served as his talisman, his charm, his link to the here and now. Equally, the dog provided a bridge to Jeremy for his friends. The customary greetings of, "Hi, how's it goin'? What's new? How ya doin'?" carried a weight of meaning if said to Jeremy, but the boys could talk to, and about, Grizzly and that carried them past initial awkwardness to casual ground. Bare acquaintances and strangers, too, admired and praised the devoted, dignified, obviously intelligent dog as a way of treating Jeremy normally while nevertheless conveying interest and concern. So well behaved was Grizzly that he was welcome wherever Jeremy went, in every house, every store, even in the downtown office where Jeremy spent hours manning a teen suicide hotline.

Jeremy's decision to volunteer at the hotline came about after a day in which he was out driving and happened upon the scene of an automobile accident. An injured, badly bleeding man was lying on the pavement and Jeremy went to him, cradled his head in his lap and talked and prayed with him, offering the man a degree of succor no one else in the gathered crowd was unself-conscious enough to tender to a stranger. Having been able to be meaningful to this stranger, who died in his arms, made Jeremy realize that his own illness need not stand in the way of his helping others. Six of his peers had died by suicide or accident in the past year or so. He was well aware that some of the kids in high school were doing drugs, that some suffered abuse in turbulent families, that some were neglected by alcoholic parents, and if there was a way to help, he wanted to do it. He talked to anyone who called the hotline, focusing on the value of life, the urgent need to appreciate it and not abuse it by resorting to alcohol or drugs or behavior that harmed body and mind.

Profoundly grateful for his own returning health, Jeremy appeared on television as co-host of a Miracle Children's Network telethon. His specific goal was to raise money for a cancer treatment center in Klamath Falls to spare future cancer victims the long trips to Portland for chemotherapy and Medford for radiation therapy, trips on which Jeremy and Lana eventually wore out a total of five secondhand cars.

In the fall, a year from the start of his illness, Jeremy resumed school. He was not able to go every day to every class but he attended some classes and then returned home, where Grizzly, with a sixth sense for his return, would be waiting at the door, sitting with ears cocked forward and tail slowly sweeping back and forth on the floor with pleasurable anticipation. The two inseparables would be off then to man the hotline, to watch football or soccer practice from the sidelines, or to head for the soothing highways, snug in the little cab and each other's company, slightly hypnotized by the unreeling of the road and the motion of the pickup. Never did Lana see the boy and the dog return home without blessing Ella Brown for the gift of companionship and love she had given Jeremy. There could not have been a richer one, and Ella in her wisdom had known it.

One day Jeremy came home from school and did not set out again. When Lana returned from the dojo late in the afternoon, his usually luminous face was gray, his eyes pale. "I don't feel very good, Mom. I think you need to take me to the doctor."

"What's going on, Jer?"

"I'm having some pain in my chest."

At the hospital a young resident studied the X rays of Jeremy's lungs, made a telephone call, and came to where Lana and Jeremy were waiting. He suggested conferring with Lana alone, but she said no, that if there were decisions to be made, Jeremy made them and he needed to know whatever there was to know. The doctor turned to Jeremy. "We need to send you back up to Portland right away."

"Oh, man," Jeremy groaned. His elbows moved to his knees and his hands covered his face. From far off came the clank of trays as a dinner wagon traveled down a corridor. Somewhere a phone rang. A nurse's sponge soles whispered past the door. Lana reached through the silence to put her hand on Jeremy's back, reached through her numbness to touch him. Jeremy pushed himself to his feet and stood very straight. In the martial arts, one sees the unseen, and Lana saw that Jeremy was marshaling the tangible and intangible forces in his world to help him fight this newly flared battle. He looked down at her and held out his hand. "Okay, Mom, let's go home and pack."

Driving home, Lana's mind revolved desperately around the problem of money. She had only a few dollars, far from enough to pay for gas to get to Portland, for food, for a place to stay. She prayed that Roger was home and had his pay in his pocket, and was relieved to see his car in the driveway. She found him in the bathroom shaving. He glanced at her as she closed the door carefully behind her; then his eyes went back to his own face in the mirror and he did not look at her again.

"Roger, I have to take Jeremy to Portland right away, tonight. The tumors are back in his lungs."

"Um."

Despairingly she said, "I didn't think this would happen so soon."

"Um."

"Roger, I don't have any money." When he said nothing, Lana assumed he had not understood. "I have to take him now, Roger. To Doernbecher. To the hospital."

"If you're asking me for money, I don't have any." As Roger tilted his chin high to shave under it, Lana slid to the floor and huddled there. All the way home she had been heading for Roger like a ship heads for port, holding herself together until his arms closed around her and he told her that he loved Jeremy and was just as afraid for him as she was, that he loved her and understood what she was going through.

Instead, Lana understood as clearly as though Roger had said so that their ten-year marriage was over, was dissolving in pain so searing that she would carry the hurt for years to come. Almost from the beginning of Jeremy's illness, Roger had been withdrawing his emotional investment in her, in Jeremy and Christen, and now she foresaw that it was only a matter of time before he left them physically as well.

The front doorbell was ringing. Lana could hear it through the crack under the bathroom door. She rolled over on her hands and knees, pushed herself to her feet, and went to answer it. Standing on the porch was a woman from their church, the Keno Christian Church. "We had a special collection on Sunday for you and Jeremy," the woman said. In the envelope was two hundred dollars.

Her voice tight with wonder, Lana asked, "How did you know to come now?" It was twilight, almost dinnertime, a time to be at home, not to travel blocks on an errand that common sense would say could perfectly well wait until morning.

"I just felt I needed to get over here with it," the woman said, and shrugged in apology for not having a better reason.

Dr. Nerhout had seen Jeremy not long before when he had generously taken time to fly to Medford to appear on the fund-raising telethon with Jeremy, and he was sad but not particularly surprised, Lana suspected, to discover him back in the hospital. As before, after he had the results of all the tests and X rays, he conferred straightforwardly with Jeremy. "We have used up all the conventional therapy," he told him. "The only thing left to try, Jer, is an experimental combination, and we don't know the side effects or what will happen with it."

"Oh, gee." An artic shiver seized Jeremy. He squeezed his eyes shut and fisted his hands. His voice came in a whisper. He cleared his throat and spoke resolutely. "How sick am I going to get this time?"

"We don't know that either, Jer. As I say, it's experimental."

"What's the treatment schedule?"

"Seven days on, seven off. Chemo one week out of every two for twelve weeks."

Jeremy whistled softly, braced his shoulders, and said what he had said those other times. "Okay, let's get started."

The surprise with this therapy was that Jeremy was not made as rackingly ill by it, but still he could not be left alone in the hospital without someone standing by to watch over him. One of the rare times Lana went out of the room when an intravenous drip was running, she was absent for just fifteen minutes and returned to find the tubing had come loose but the needle remained in Jeremy's arm and his bright blood was pumping in a pulsing stream into the bedclothes and pooling on the floor. After that, she did not feel she could leave Jeremy even at night, and she was soon drowning in a sea of exhaustion. The only relief was when Eric Lund came, as before, on weekends and when Susanne could get away from her job and travel down from Seattle.

The weeks went by in a daze of treatments and drives back and forth between Portland and Klamath Falls or, later in the winter when the mountain passes were blocked by snow, borrowed airplane rides patched together from whatever company, private, or Lifeflight jet Lana could beg to take them. Somewhere in this time Lana collapsed, and now it was she racing toward the hospital on a stretcher in a screaming, red-blinking ambulance. Residents and nurses swarmed over her; she was hitched up to monitors, machines beeped, alarms went off, people ran.

"I can't be sick! I can't be in the hospital!"

"You've had a heart attack, Mrs. Stewart."

"No!"

"You had a heart attack at home and two more in the ambulance on the way here."

"I have to get Jeremy to Portland for his chemotherapy treatments or he will die!"

"Mrs. Stewart, you have had three heart attacks—"

"No! No!"

To assess the extent of the damage to her heart, her attending physician had Lana transported by ambulance to Medford for a cardiac catheterization. On the hour-long trip, Lana prayed—her children needed her now more than ever; she could not be sick—but her prayers were oddly peaceful, quite as though she knew the doctors would find nothing. And she was right. There had been no heart attacks. The cause of her symptoms was Graves' disease, a condition in which the thyroid gland becomes hyperactive, churning out so much thyroid hormone that the heart pounds unmercifully and the breath comes in short gasps. Radioactive isotope treatment knocked out the gland, and Lana escaped from the hospital and hitched a ride on a plane back to Klamath Falls just in time for the next trip to Portland.

In January the experimental course of treatment was over, and Jeremy and Lana went back to Klamath Falls to give him time to regain some strength. In February, after Jeremy's blood count came back up, they returned to Portland for Jeremy to have a CAT scan, bone scan, and bone-marrow biopsy to determine whether the treatment had been effective. After the tests came another day's wait for the results. At the end of the day they were summoned to Dr. Nerhout's offce.

The answer, read by Jeremy as quickly as by Lana, was written on Dr. Nerhout's face. "I'm so sorry, Jer," he said quietly. "I wanted to be able to give you good news, but I can't." He put X rays of Jeremy's lungs on the light box and pointed out the tumors, fourteen of them. "The treatment didn't work."

"Not at all?"

"Not at all."

Jeremy accepted the words, nodded, nodded again, looking at some indeterminate spot on the floor. Lana put out her hand.

He squeezed it and let it go. "Well, all right," he said carefully, "what else can we try?"

"I'm afraid there's nothing."

Jeremy's head came up sharply. "C'mon, there must be something we can do. It's not that I'm afraid to die but I'm not finished fighting this disease."

"Jer, there are no options left."

Suddenly Jeremy was angry. "I won't let you wimp out on me. Ask some other experts. Call other hospitals. Find out about other things. Experiment on me. I can take it."

"I'm sorry, Jer. The only thing that makes sense now is for you to go home and be with your family, your dog, see your friends, have fun."

"You can't give up on me. I won't let you! I'm a fighter."

"Jeremy, you have no chance of surviving."

There it was at last. As unequivocal as a fist in the face, as final as a slamming door. Jeremy, you are sixteen and your life is ending. Lana, your son is going to die. On smoothly oiled chains, the drawbridge to life was being drawn up and Jeremy and Lana were left behind, marooned on an island of aloneness. Lana heard a strange, strangled sound, as though a kitten was trapped beneath a floorboard. She turned to look for it. Then she realized the sound was coming from her.

"When?" Jeremy asked Dr. Nerhout.

"Three months. Six months."

Jeremy stood up. "When I'm ready to quit fighting, I'll know and I'll let you know."

Lana followed Jeremy out of Dr. Nerhout's office and down the corridor, both of them wordless and tearless. They had gone past any ordinary place where there were words, where there were tears.

At the door to his hospital room, Jeremy said, "Mom, I want a milkshake."

"Okay."

"I want to go with you to get it."

"Okay."

The nurses at the station said, "We haven't seen you leave, Jer. Come back whenever you feel like it."

They drove to a Dairy Queen. Jeremy went to the window, ordered his milkshake, and brought it back to the car. He had almost finished it when Lana said, "I love you, Jer."

"I know that, Mom. I've always known that." The straw sucked the bottom of the milkshake dry. "I love you too."

He got out to throw the container away. When he came back, Lana said, "Do you want to drive?"

"You'd better. I'm kind of tired."

At the hospital they learned that Kennon had been brought in and was asking to see Jeremy. Kennon was a boy three years younger than Jeremy, a boy from a broken home who lived with his sister and her family in Klamath Falls. When Kennon was diagnosed with an osteosarcoma of his thigh bone, the school principal suggested, "Go talk to Jeremy," and Jeremy had struggled hard to transfuse courage and fight and hopefulness into Kennon, arranging whenever possible for them to be in the hospital for chemotherapy at the same time so that Kennon would have someone to be with and talk to. This night the nurses said Kennon had had a setback and was scheduled for emergency surgery in the morning.

"You can't go to him," Lana told Jeremy. "You can hardly breathe and you're in major pain, I can see it in your eyes."

"Mom, he's scared. I have you, but Kennon doesn't have anyone."

Lana went on to Jeremy's room alone. Susanne, knowing they would have news that day, had driven from Seattle after work and was waiting in the chair by the bed. Seeing her there, having her arms go around her, broke through Lana's numbness. "Oh, Sue, they can't fix what's wrong!" The tears came in a flood now, Lana's tears and Susanne's. When she could speak, Lana said, "Darling, thank you for coming."

"I love him too. And you." She studied Lana's face. "I think you need to be by yourself tonight," she said. "Go back to your room. I'll stay with Jer."

"Watch him closely. Get the nurses if anything happens."

It was around midnight when Lana got to her room at the Ronald McDonald House, but it was not sleep she hungered for. Understanding? She would never understand why her child had to die. Solace? There was none for what was coming. Release? Yes, something like that perhaps. She sat down at a little table in the room and began to write furiously, screaming out her feelings on paper, scrawled page after scrawled page of inchoate, untargeted resentment, confusion, rebellion, anger at the sharp-toothed unkindness of fate, at the pestilential unfairness of greedy, mindless cells growing fat as mushrooms in the twin caves of her son's lungs, at the coming end by cruel and dreadful stealth of his precious life.

At four in the morning came a hammering on the door. A policeman loomed there. "An emergency at the hospital, Mrs. Stewart. They have to do a procedure on your son, and they need you to sign a permission form. Throw a coat on and I'll take you over."

At the hospital Lana ran through the halls, crashed through the double doors to the pediatric wing, fought through the white-coated backs crowded into Jeremy's room. "Let me in! Let me in!"

"You can't come in now."

"I'm his mother. You have to let me in!"

Sue, huddled in a corner, turned stricken eyes on Lana. Jeremy was bent over the side of the bed, a doctor supporting him, another doctor wielding a hypodermic as big as a knitting needle, a third doctor holding a bottle for fluid to flow into. The doctor with the huge needle jabbed it into Jeremy's back, moved it around with repeated small jabs, pulled it out, and slammed it in again.

"What's happened? What's going on?" Lana demanded frantically.

"Oh, Mom," Jeremy moaned.

A doctor said, "We have to do this."

"Can't you give him an anesthetic?"

"No. This is an emergency. He can't breathe. His lungs are filled with fluid."

Jeremy, age three.

Jeremy riding his dirt bike.

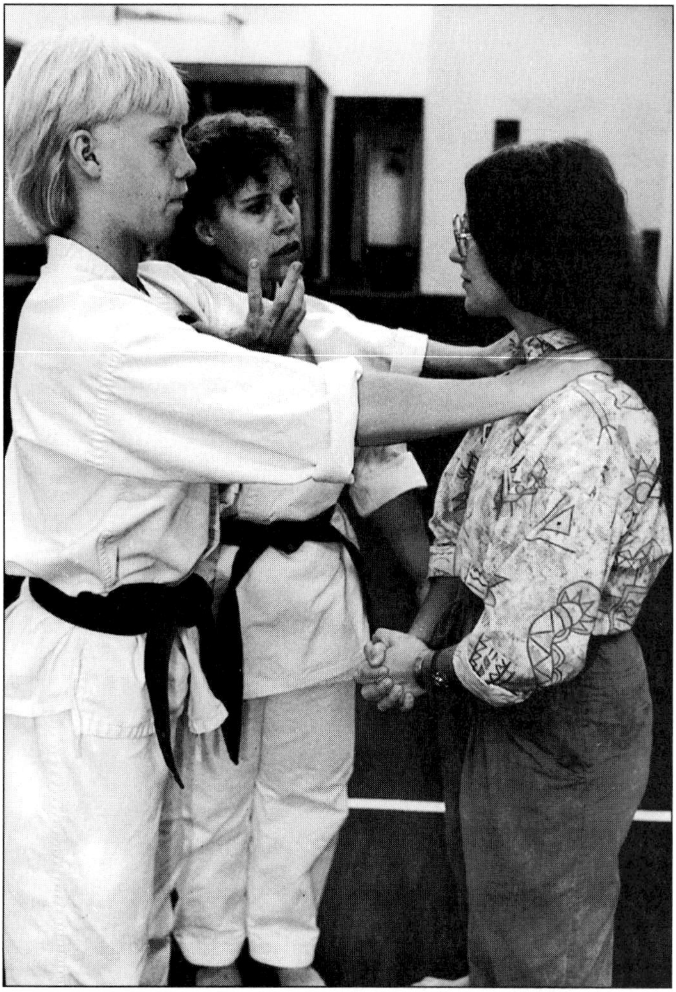

Jeremy and Lana teaching self-defense class at the dojo in 1987.

Jeremy sparring in competition.

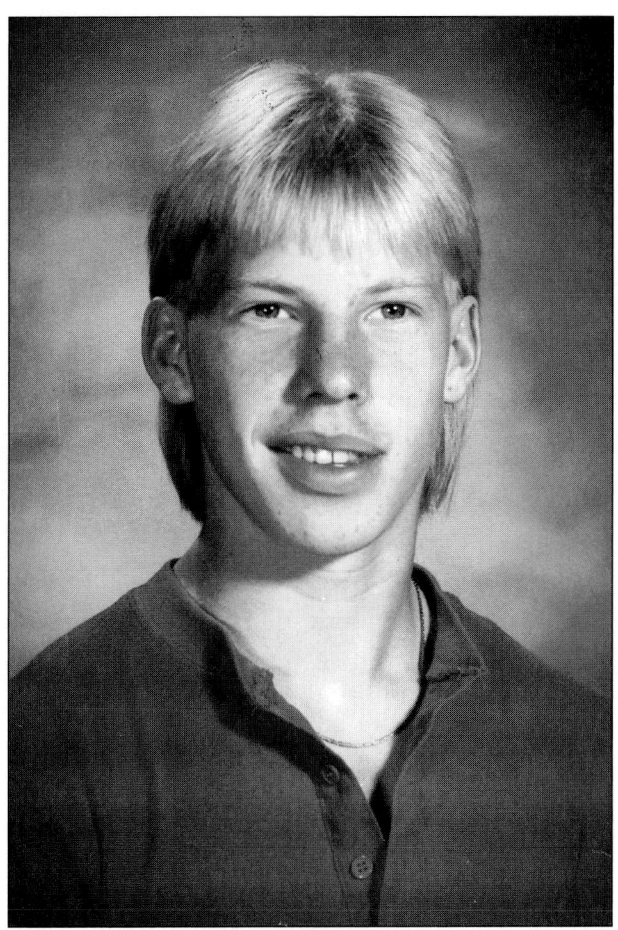

Jeremy, October 1987 (age fifteen).

Jeremy in October, just before he was hurt.

Eric Lund, Jeremy's best friend, with Jeremy's sister, Christen, waiting to go on TV in Medford, Oregon.

Jeremy and the governor of Oregon raising funds for a cancer treatment center in Klamath Falls, June 1988.

photo by Christopher Briscoe

Jeremy co-hosting the Children's Miracle Network telethon to raise money for kids and hospitals.

Jeremy and his sisters, Susanne (age nineteen) and Christen (age thirteen), in February 1988. This photo, taken shortly after learning that Jeremy's illness was terminal, typifies Jeremy's relationship with his sisters, who adored him, and the intense closeness they shared.

Ella Brown with Grizzly's father, Rainy Ridge, Grizzly himself, and Grizzly's grandmother at Ella's kennel.

Jeremy and his best friend, Eric Lund, in 1988 at the dojo, after Jeremy awarded Eric his green belt. Jeremy had recently undergone extensive chemotherapy treatments when this photo was taken. All his hair was gone, which is why he is wearing a bandanna.

Jeremy at home with Grizzly two months before he died.

Jeremy and friends with his beloved blue truck six weeks before he died. Photo taken on Jeremy's seventeenth birthday, March 13, as the boys prepared for Jeremy's big snowboarding trip. From left to right: Jeremy, Shawn Richards, Jason Titus, and Adam Hart.

Grizzly, Jeremy, and friends Adam Hart, Jason Titus, Allan Dotson, and Eric Lund. Jason was a big guy who carried Jeremy around when he couldn't walk.

Jeremy just learning to snowboard. He was able to stay up on his first attempt.

Lana and Grizzly on their first trip "home" to Klamath Falls after they had moved to Utah, eighteen months after Jeremy died. Amazingly, after all that time away, Grizzly found Jeremy's grave site almost immediately.

Grizzly prompting Lana to keep walking in 1990 against the backdrop of Utah's Wasatch Range. Grizzly had insisted that Lana begin walking again after months of near seclusion. When Lana would try to turn back, he would look at her and encourage her to take a few more steps. "He had much to show me ahead, and he would patiently wait for me, then start out again and show me the way to go, just as he later showed me the direction my life should take."

Lana and Dave's wedding reception in 1989, near Seattle. Clockwise: Lana, Dave, Susie, Lana's mother Magdalene Wilcox, and Christen.

Lana moved around in front of Jeremy. He looked at her and his sky-blue eyes were white, his skin cold and wet. His head fell forward on her shoulder.

"Okay, Jer," the doctor with the needle said, "one more time and we're in." He rammed the needle home between two ribs.

Jeremy screamed and fainted on Lana's shoulder. She supported his body while still the doctor probed and probed. Finally the doctor admitted, "I just can't get it."

"Then get out."

A small amount of red-tinged fluid drained into the bottle. "I need to get more," the doctor muttered.

"No," Lana commanded. "Pull that needle out right now and get out of here. All of you! Just get out!"

The doctor withdrew the needle, and as it came out, Jeremy regained consciousness. The medical people laid him on the bed and left the room. Lana wanted to run down the hall screaming but first she had to comfort Jeremy, arrange his pillows to prop him up to breathe, settle the covers around him, dry his face. "Stay with him," she told Sue. "I'll be right back."

She found an empty room and beat her fists on the bed. "How much does he have to go through? I can't bear it! I can't bear it!" She was sobbing when Sue came to find her, only the thinnest of sinews still holding her together after a fashion. Sue picked up the telephone and called Klamath Falls. Christen answered, and Sue told her to get Roger. At first, Roger refused to come to the phone, and when he did, he said only, "Why did you get me out of bed?" and hung up. Sue then dialed Salt Lake City where Dave Davis lived. Dave was someone Lana had known before she married Roger. His mother and Lana's mother were friends, and he had had news of Jeremy from her. Not wanting to bother Lana, he had occasionally been telephoning Susanne to ask for word on Jeremy's condition. Now she said to him, "Dave, I'm sorry to wake you up but my mom needs someone to talk to."

Lana could hardly speak, but Dave was patient and asked what had happened, going from small question to small question until she had described all the terrors of this awful day and night. He did not say much—what was there to say?—but it helped that he was there listening. Lana thanked him, and Sue talked to him a bit more while Lana went back to Jeremy's room to watch over him.

In the morning there was a message from Dave Davis. He had made a plane reservation to fly in from Utah and would be in Portland that afternoon.

Sue was glad to have him there; he was someone older and steadying for her to lean on, a solid person. He visited Jeremy on each of the three days he stayed, and although Lana had not seen him in twelve years and supposed that politeness required she should be reestablishing contact, she so needed to snatch moments for herself that she took advantage of his visits to walk outside, to look at the sky, to stare into faces, to take in the dimensions of that other world outside the world of the hospital. She was aware of Dave's kindness and strength but only passingly aware of him as a person.

He left, and Sue left too, and Lana stayed on while Jeremy underwent daily radiation treatments for six weeks to reduce the size of the tumors in his lungs to allow for somewhat easier breathing. On the last day of treatment, Jeremy said, "Mom, take me home. I want to die at home."

"You're sure, Jer?"

"If I've got to die, I want to do it at home. I'm sick of this. Please, Mom, take me home."

Hours later, they were on the road, on their last drive back from Portland to Klamath Falls.

Lana had telephoned ahead that they were coming, but Roger seemed surprised to see them. "I didn't expect you this early," he said. "I'm on my way to teach at the dojo." He looked at Jeremy but said nothing before he got in his truck and drove off.

Inside the house, Lana saw that it had not been cleaned in the six weeks she had been away. Christen had gone to live with friends, and Roger had simply piled dirty dishes and pots and pans in the sink and on the counters. Green mold was growing everywhere. Newspapers were strewn about. Muddy footprints tracked over the rugs. In their bedroom, dirty underwear, dirty shirts, dirty jeans lay in piles on the floor. Bureau drawers hung open. The sheets on the bed were gray.

When Roger came home that night, Lana exploded. Roger's answer was, "If you don't like it here, leave."

"No," said Lana. "No. If anyone is going to leave, it will be you."

She went to bed on the living room couch that night. The following evening when Roger came home, he brought several church leaders with him, and Lana quickly realized that the reason they were there was to convince her to accept marriage counseling. Unable to deal with what was happening to Jeremy, Roger had focused on the marriage. Defining it as broken, he considered that it was up to Lana to fix it, and the leaders assured Lana that Roger was willing to offer her a bargain: he would stay if she agreed to work on the marriage.

Lana stared disbelievingly at the men. "My son is upstairs dying. I haven't slept for six weeks straight. And you want me to do what? You have to be crazy!"

The men shifted uneasily but stood their ground. "Don't you want to save your marriage?"

Lana turned to Roger. "Any work on this marriage is going to have to wait until Jeremy is dead. In the meantime, if you want to help me, fine. If not, I want you out of here. I'm tired. I'm scared. I need some peace. And my son is not going to die in the midst of selfish, quarreling adults!"

The next day Roger was gone. So that was the answer to whether he could stay the course or whether, like fully half the fathers of children in the hospital, he could not bear the stress of a fatal illness in the family. Lana supposed she understood—at least her mind did—but she had loved him dearly and she was devastated that he had failed her and failed Jeremy.

4
The Running Shoes

It was February when Jeremy went home to die. In March he would have his seventeenth birthday, and his most passionate wish was for a snowboard. Roger, when Lana asked for his help, snorted over the idiocy of paying two hundred dollars for a snowboard for a dying boy and flatly refused to consider it. Lana did not have two hundred dollars; indeed, she had had to apply for food stamps in order for them to have something to eat. Word of Jeremy's wish reached their church and the members set to work to try to raise the money, but before they had quite achieved their goal, United Parcel Service delivered a package containing the best snowboard that money could buy. It was a gift from Dave Davis in Utah, who had heard from Susanne that this was what Jeremy so dearly wanted. The money the church raised then enabled Lana to take Jeremy downtown and outfit him in pants, jacket, boots, gloves, and goggles. Thus equipped, off Jeremy went with his friends on his birthday to Mount Ashland, where the best hotel donated two rooms for their stay, one for Lana and Christen, the other for the five boys. Jeremy, still the graceful natural athlete, caught on to snowboarding as effortlessly as he had gotten the hang of surfboarding, and he and the boys were on the slopes until a whiteout drove them, wet, tired, hungry, and happy, into the lodge. There a television crew that had been following the boys through much of the day finally had a chance to interview Jeremy.

In response to a question or two, Jeremy faced the camera and said what was on his mind to an unseen audience, particularly to an audience of teenagers: "I'm not worried about dying. Dying will take care of itself. I'm working on living, and what I've learned about living is this: You have to be supportive of each other, not turn your back on someone because he looks different or weaker. You have to respect other people. Respect your parents and your own life. You have to respect your body. Take care of it. Keep it fit. Drugs and drinking are not the answer to anything. Being a man, being macho, has nothing to do with drugs and alcohol and smoking and sex. Those things'll weaken you, pull you down. You have to work hard. Work hard and don't give up. That way you'll have value, you'll achieve something with your life."

Back home, Jeremy and his friends relived the thrills of that weekend as they lounged in the living room after school hours or took Jeremy for drives or went downtown for Cokes, always with Grizzly by Jeremy's side. But by the end of April, it taxed Jeremy's strength just to get downstairs, and he made the effort only for the comfort and distraction of watching television. The one set in the house, a twenty-inch one, was in the living room and Jeremy was watching an *I Love Lucy* rerun late one day when the front door opened and in stalked Roger. Saying only, "I'm taking this," Roger strode across the room, pulled the plug from the wall, and hoisted up the set. Lana, hearing the heavy footsteps, hurried in from the kitchen.

"Roger!"

"I paid for it, I'm takin' it."

"But Roger, Jeremy—"

"Never mind, Mom," Jeremy said. "Let him have it. It doesn't matter."

Roger backed out the door, leaving it open. Jeremy got up to close it, then made his way up to his room. He never came downstairs again.

Lana went to the police and had Roger served with a restraining order so he could not take anything else from the house, and shortly after that Roger had her served with divorce papers. With Jeremy now too ill to get out of bed and in increasingly harsh pain, Lana was frantic with concern for him. The papers, as devastating as they might have been at another time, seemed less a blow than a distraction. She asked her friend Martha Freeman, who was spending days at the dining room table sorting through the shoebox of bills and dealing with insurance forms, to look them over to tell her if there was anything in them that sounded unreasonable. Since there did not seem to be, Lana signed them unread.

As the last swift downhill run gathered momentum, Jeremy asked Lana for paper and a pen so that he could make out his will. He left his possessions—his snowboard, his little blue pickup, his trophies—to his friends. His most important possession he left to Lana. "Mom, I want you to have Grizzly," he told her. "Maybe there's a way for you and Griz to help other sick kids." He added thoughtfully, "Be sure to tell Ella how much I thank her. By giving me Grizzly, she helped me to know what it would have been like to be a father."

Grizzly spent his days and nights by Jeremy's side, lying quietly on the bed when Jeremy wanted to rest against him, lying on the floor next to the bed when Jeremy was struggling to breathe. Lana was either in the room or connected to it by a monitor that let her know instantly if Jeremy needed her. As his condition worsened and his breathing grew more labored, not wanting her son to die alone in the night, Lana took to sleeping in the small room on the floor beside his bed. With the snowboard leaning against the wall where Jeremy's eyes could rest on it and he could relive the thrill of swooping down the mountain slopes, there was little free space, so Lana lay there, spoon fashion, curled around Grizzly.

The night before Jeremy died, Lana lay on the floor in such emotional pain that her stomach felt tied in aching knots. Grizzly came to her and talked softly in his throat, nuzzling under her chin, then settling next to her, pressing against her, which eased the pain in her stomach. With her arm around him and his warmth stealing through her, Lana was able to relax slightly, and so they stayed through the night, Grizzly never moving, not an inch, as though by lying so uncharacteristically still he could draw the pain out of Lana and take it into himself.

The next afternoon, cradled in Lana's arms, Jeremy's breaths grew shallow, shuddered, speeded up; slowed, stopped for almost a minute; speeded up, slowed, stopped; speeded up, slowed, stopped. Stopped. Stopped—and did not come again. Jeremy was gone. The long fight was over.

Grizzly rushed from the room, down the stairs, and whined so urgently at the front door that a neighbor arriving to see if she could be of help to Lana opened the door and let him out. No one watched him go because, by that time, Jeremy's body was being carried downstairs and out to the ambulance waiting to take the body to the funeral home. Some moments later a stranger came to the door, leading Grizzly. "I was driving past," he said, "when this dog dashed out of the house and ran into the side of my car. I didn't hit him, he hit me. It was as though he didn't even know the car was there."

Grizzly showed no obvious signs of being hurt, and Ella came and took him to the kennel to relieve Lana of concern for him while she arranged for Jeremy's funeral. Lana said to the minister, "Jeremy and Grizzly were so close that I can't imagine Grizzly not being at the funeral. Would it be all right if I asked Ella to bring him?" The minister understood and agreed.

Jeremy, wanting there to be upbeat, happy music at his funeral, had asked to have Lana and two of his friends play and the high school choir sing. Lana was playing the prelude music on the piano and hundreds of people had filed in, filling the church to overflowing, when Ella and Grizzly entered and walked up the center aisle. Grizzly wore a collar of blue flowers a florist had made for him. Pacing slowly, with dignity, he led Ella to the casket at the front of the church, sniffed, and spoke so softly in his throat that only Ella heard him. Then he turned and followed Ella into a pew, crawled under it, and lay unmoving throughout the service. When the service ended and the casket was wheeled down the aisle with six of Jeremy's friends flanking it as pall-bearers, Grizzly emerged from under the pew and fell into step behind them, following the boy he loved on their final walk together. At the cemetery he remained with Jeremy's friends through the graveside service, unleashed, unheld, no hand on his head or collar, until all the words had been said and the casket had been lowered into the grave, then he went to Ella.

When Ella let him out of the car at the kennel, Grizzly ignored the other dogs and set to work digging a hole under the building. When it was large enough and deep enough, he crawled into it. There he stayed.

He was still there three days later when Lana came. Lana was leaving Klamath Falls. Roger had divorced her, the decree becoming final two days before Jeremy died. She had no money to pay the rent on the house or buy food, she was too sick, too fogged with grief to work, and a couple who had offered her a room in their house suddenly had to withdraw the offer when their daughter changed her mind about going away to college. Lana asked her sister in Kansas to take Christen and she herself planned to go to Susanne's in Seattle until she could think where to live, what to do, and how to begin patching a life together out of the ruins.

"Grizzly's under the kennel," Ella told her. "He's been there ever since the funeral."

"Without food?"

Ella nodded. "He won't even come out for water. Animals can grieve just as fiercely as we do. Grizzly's grieving for Jeremy."

Lana and Ella walked back to the kennel. Kneeling on the packed dirt next to the hole Grizzly had clawed out, Lana spoke lovingly and low, tears mingling with her words, until finally she heard the scrape of Grizzly backing out of the hole. The dog emerged, his fur matted and dirty, his body caved in around the cage of his ribs, his eyes not meeting hers as he rested his head against her knee.

"Ella," Lana said, "he's going to die."

"I'm afraid so."

Coaxing, scolding, her hand imperative on his neck ruff, Lana led the dog step by halting step to the house and into Ella's kitchen. "What am I going to do?" Lana asked Ella. "I can't take him to Seattle with me."

"He won't make it if he stays here," Ella said. "He needs a family, a home."

Lana looked into the dog's sunken eyes, at the tail that did not thump even when she spoke to him. A home, a family, someone to care for him. Jeremy had left Grizzly to her and she was not going to be able to save him any more than she had been able to save her son. Was she even going to be able to save herself? Nothing held her world together now. She was at the end of her rope and she could imagine no way to tie a knot in it and hang on. She wanted to put her head down on Ella's kitchen table, sleep, and not wake up.

As Ella, sensing this, put out a hand and covered Lana's, the face of Dave Davis came into Lana's mind. He had come to see Jeremy in the hospital, he had sent the snowboard, he had been the person sustaining Susanne through the difficult days, he had said, "If there's anything I can do . . ." What had Susanne told her about him? That he was living in a suburb of Salt Lake City, that he had a house and a yard and a dog named Tiffany.

"Call him," Ella said.

"He won't be home in the middle of the afternoon." But Lana picked up the phone anyway, tracked his number down through Directory Assistance, and dialed. Dave answered on the first ring. He had come home to pick up some software needed in his office, had just collected it, and was walking out the door when the phone rang. "Dave," Lana said, "Jeremy gave me Grizzly, his German shepherd, and I'm . . ." She faltered.

"I can hear how you are," Dave said gently.

"I'm not able to take care of him right now. The dog's in pretty bad shape, too, and I was wondering if you could look after him for a while until I can get a place of my own."

"Sure. Tiffy's a good girl and she loves to mother puppies and kittens. I'm sure she'd accept Grizzly. But how can we get him here?"

"I could ship him by plane, I suppose, if I can find some way to borrow the money."

Ella held out her hand for the phone. "Let me talk to him." She asked Dave for his address and how large his yard was and was it fenced and what breed of dog Tiffany was. "Well, Dave, it sounds as though your place is where Grizzly should be. I'll tell you what, I'm going to be driving to a dog show in Salt Lake City next week. Suppose I bring Grizzly to you? Give me directions how to get to your house." After she had written the information down and arranged a day and time, she hung up and turned to Lana. "Okay, we're all set."

Lana hugged her wordlessly. She suspected—she was almost certain—that there was no dog show in Salt Lake City the following weekend and that Ella was intending to drive hundreds of miles across parts of Oregon and Utah and all of Nevada simply to deliver Grizzly to a place where, with luck and care, he might have a chance of surviving.

She herself somehow made it to Seattle and Susanne's apartment where, sick at heart, sick in body with Graves' disease, she collapsed. After a week, desperate for money to pay for the medical treatment she knew she needed, she struggled downtown one afternoon to apply for work at an agency dealing in temporary workers. Because of her manual dexterity as a pianist, she was a rapid and accurate typist and had no trouble being put on the roster of secretaries for hire. Rather than this giving her spirits a lift, however, on the drive home she stopped at a traffic light and suddenly, as though a sluice gate had been opened, torrents of tears descended. The light changed, and changed again, horns honked, drivers stared curiously as they pulled around her, and still she could not drive on. Grief was a quicksand in which she was sinking. Her muscles quivered and were useless. Only when the gruff voice of a policeman shouted at her to move on was she able to start the car up again.

When finally she made it back to Susanne's apartment, the telephone was ringing. Dave Davis was calling from Utah to report on Grizzly. As Lana listened, her tears continued to fall like rain, running down her face as rapidly and silently as drops on a windshield. It was beyond her ability to stop them and had nothing to do with

Dave's news. He was describing how Tiffy, his black Labrador, had intuited how near death Grizzly was and made room for him on her dog bed, lay close to warm him, washed him with her soft tongue, and nosed him to her water and food bowls. Grizzly, too weak to walk when he arrived, had managed a painfully slow half-block excursion with Dave and Tiffy the evening before, and that was the good news Dave was calling to report. He did not hang up then but with quiet, persistent questions pried open Lana's despair and learned as well of her physical illness. He kept her on the phone for two hours, talking inconsequentially through Lana's silences, waiting through her sudden storms of sobs, finally saying to her, "Lana, I don't want to step out of bounds here, but it sounds like you could use a break and a friend. What would you think about coming out to Utah for a couple of weeks to stay with Griz and Tiffy and me? The Gina Bachauer Piano Festival is starting here in a few days, and you could go listen to some of the finest pianists in the world. I have a spare bedroom and bathroom, so you'd have all the privacy you need. Suppose I send a plane ticket tomorrow? If you decide not to use it, you can cash it in and have a bit of money, but it would be best if you came and let me take care of you."

Lana accepted the ticket and flew to Utah. In the darkened spare bedroom of Dave's house, she slept hours every morning while Dave was at work at the software company where he wrote technical manuals, and in the afternoons a friend of his picked her up and drove her to the festival, where the music poured into Lana, sometimes liquid, sometimes percussive, sometimes stirring her pain, sometimes soothing it. In the early evening, when Dave came home, he took the dogs walking in the fields at the base of a nearby mountain. He was never impatient, always kind, never demanding, always gentle, tactful, accepting, content to have Lana be there, content to have her exist in whatever limbo she inhabited. He did not suggest or recommend or urge. He did not offer advice. He attempted neither to cheer nor encourage her. He did that unusual thing: he let her be.

When the two weeks of the festival were over, Lana flew back to Seattle, leaving Grizzly with Dave and Tiffy. Dave telephoned often to report on Grizzly's progress and to listen quietly while Lana struggled to sort through her thoughts and find a direction for her life to take. In one of their conversations a month after Lana had been living at Susanne's, Dave asked Lana to marry him.

"I know we haven't had time to build the kind of relationship most couples have when they marry," he said, "but you need caring for just as much as Grizzly and I think we can be good for each other."

Lana groaned, not for any particular reason except that the thought of making an effort of any sort was beyond her. She still was not sure how to respond a week later when they talked again. "Let's talk about some of the reasons why marrying me makes sense," Dave said. "You need a place to live and you need to make a home for Christen. You'd have both here. You need really good medical care, and you have no money and no insurance. I can take care of that; I can easily support you and Christen. And, of course, there is the most important reason of all: Tiffy needs to have Grizzly to look after. She hasn't been so happy in years." He chuckled in case Lana did not realize this last was a joke.

From deep within the cave where that person who was herself was crouched, still existing but profoundly numb, Lana said, "You're right, Dave, I need, I need, I need. But there is nothing in me to give."

"I won't ask you for anything."

"You've fed me, held me, been the best friend I've ever had. But in a year or two, or next week, perhaps I'll look at you and say, Who is this? What is he doing in my life?"

"If that happens, you're absolutely free to walk away. I'll say, that's okay, and it will be okay."

"I died with Jeremy. I've lost my soul. I'm an empty shell. I'm in no condition to care about anyone. I'm not capable of it. I can't love another man. I loved Roger with all my heart. He's gone. My son is gone. Everyone I love is gone."

"You need a home and a friend. That is all I am offering you."

It was not decided then or on any particular day following, but it came to be accepted that the marriage, because it provided necessary answers for Lana, would come about, not because she willed it or wanted it, not because it provided a way back to life for her, but simply because she gave it no thought, and because she did not refuse or argue against it, it came to seem agreed upon. And one day it happened, in July of 1989, at the home of a cousin of Lana's in a suburb of Seattle, although Lana could not remember afterward if it had happened in her imagination or in actuality.

Back in Utah, Dave showed her the marriage license when she asked, but she forgot she had seen it and asked again, not caring what the answer was. Her days passed lying in bed, existing in a barren landscape of grayness and holding herself still against the aching of the wasted muscles in her arms and legs and the grip of pain on her heart. When Dave came home in the evening, he fed the dogs and made supper for Lana, taking it to her on a tray. While she ate, and often again at bedtime, he read to her—at first, books as simple as *Yertle the Turtle;* next, Dickens's *Great Expectations;* and then Edith Wharton's *The Age of Innocence.* Gradually, Lana became able to listen, to hear the words and fit them together into sense, to forget herself, to forget her sorrow for minutes at a time.

The specialist Dave took Lana to stabilized her thyroid condition and made the additional diagnoses of post-traumatic stress syndrome and chronic fatigue syndrome, for which he had no answers. She was in almost constant pain, and it did not seem worthwhile to her to try to distinguish what proportion was mental and what physical.

One day the pain finally became too great. Lana dragged herself to the bathroom, closed her hand around a bottle of Demerol prescribed for Jeremy, and crept back to sit on the edge of the bed. Grizzly, hearing her move around, had come into the room and was watching her. He put his head in her lap, his dark, wise eyes steadily on her as her tears rained down on his head. Lana kissed him goodbye and took the lid off the bottle. Grizzly jerked his head up. The bottle flew out of Lana's hand. The pills scattered over the floor in every direction. As Lana stared at them, Grizzly brought his head up to her face and woofed sharply.

His bark was serious. Lana had the impression that he was not pleading, not arguing with her, not begging; he was telling her that he would not let her do this. *Look at me,* he seemed to be saying. *Look at me. I loved Jeremy too, but I'm healing. So can you. Your life is too valuable to throw away.*

The message he was sending was so powerful, so unmistakable, that Lana was stunned. Grizzly, never taking his eyes off her while she gathered up the pills, backed away until he was at the bathroom door and gave two imperious barks. Lana followed him into the bathroom as though under orders. Grizzly stood by the toilet and again sounded a dictatorial bark. Obediently, Lana emptied the pills into the toilet and flushed it.

She went back to bed and Grizzly jumped up and stretched out full length beside her, sheltering her with the warmth of his body. And there he stayed until Dave came home.

Lana was so weak she could barely climb a flight of steps, and never without stopping to rest two or three times. Every muscle and joint in her body ached, her throat hurt, her stomach pained so that, for a full year, she slept with a pillow pressed against her abdomen. Mornings she saw Christen off to school and did a bare minimum of housework—washed the breakfast dishes, dusted, ran the vacuum in one room—and then crawled back into bed and slept for four or five hours, although she dreaded sleep because of the horror of her dreams. Sometimes she sat on the living room couch, staring through the glass doors to the deck and the lawn beyond, watching Tiffy and Grizzly play or looking out as the two dogs lay on the deck, Tiffy washing Grizzly's face until it shone. Lana felt disconnected, an alien from life or, when the tears flowed down her face, an object as inanimate as a rain barrel filled to overflowing. Her tears were soundless, but Grizzly always knew. He would come through the pet door, which allowed the dogs to go in and out at will, and move to her to lick away her tears. At such times Lana hugged him and talked about Jeremy, what a great boy he had been, how much she missed him, and Grizzly sang a little chirking song with his muzzle tucked between her shoulder and neck to comfort her.

One afternoon as she lay in the shadowed bedroom, she heard a persistent small sound, a wooden scrape of the sliding closet door. She opened her eyes and saw that Grizzly had come into the room. With his nose and a paw, he was working at the door, bumping it against a stopper as he labored to slide it open. Discovering that too strong an effort jammed the door, he eased up and worked it open an inch at a time until he could get his head through. Lana heard his snuffle as he rooted in the bottom of the closet. When he found what he was after, he backed out resolutely, Lana's running shoe in his mouth. Delicately he laid the shoe on the pillow beside her head, backed off, waved his tail slowly, then turned and retrieved the second shoe from the closet. It too was laid on the pillow. Again his tail waved, not eagerly but encouragingly, and he woofled deep in his throat.

Lana summoned the will to ask, "Do you have to go out?" Grizzly half turned to the door in assent. Feeling as though she were moving underwater with weights attached to her limbs, Lana struggled up from the bed, made her way to the door opening on the deck, and slid it back for Grizzly to go through. Grizzly looked up at her and did not move. "Go on," she said. "You can go out by yourself." He took a step backward and woofled. "Grizzly, go!" she ordered. He backed up farther and again spoke in his throat. "Are you hungry? Thirsty?" But the water bowl was full and he ignored the dog biscuit she held out. "I give up," she told him irritably. "I don't know what you want."

The dog followed her back to the bedroom and watched as she threw the running shoes into the closet, slid the door closed, and dropped down on the bed, where she lay curled on her side. Grizzly put his large head in the curve of her body and made little grieving whimpers in the depths of his throat.

"Go away," Lana told him. "Leave me alone."

The next afternoon the same sounds penetrated the tomb of grief where Lana lay lifeless. Again Grizzly nosed out her running shoes and placed them on the pillow beside her, backed off, spoke, and wagged his tail in slow, hopeful arcs. Now Lana understood. "You want me to go out. You think it's time for me to stop lying here." Grizzly snapped his teeth in assent. Lana sat up on the side of the bed and Grizzly put his head in her lap. Her tears fell on him but he did not try to avoid them, existing there with her until Lana fell back on the bed and curled up again.

On the third day, when Grizzly brought her running shoes, Lana put them on and made it as far as the living room couch before collapsing. Grizzly settled on the floor beside her, not badgering her, seemingly content with this small step. On the fourth day Lana made it outside and walked half a block, Grizzly at her side, brushing against her reassuringly when she staggered and making no objection when she turned around after such a brief outing.

And so it went, each day a little farther, now with Grizzly loping ahead but constantly checking to see if Lana was following and making no objection, showing no disappointment, when she turned to go home again. He understood, as Tiffy had understood with him, that Lana could be led back to life only little by little, that strength would return only bit by bit, that the will was a fragile thing to be coaxed, never commanded. Grizzly seemed to know, too, as he had known with Jeremy, when Lana was physically ill and when it was depression that anchored her to the bed. He sat by the bed, his chin resting on it, sounding his encouraging grunts, chirks, whimpers, and woofs and now and again clicking his teeth when it was fog that Lana was lost in. But when the pain was physical, he lay quietly beside the bed, there for her, being there with her, but accepting and quiet.

Every day for a year Grizzly continued the ritual of fetching Lana's shoes and insisting on a walk. At the end of the year Lana had regained enough strength to walk for an hour, leave the suburban streets behind, and wander where Grizzly led, through fields of wildflowers and onto the sandy plateaus under the steep mountains.

She was picking yellow daisies one warm spring day when Grizzly came to her and touched her. "What's going on, Griz?" He froze and pointed like a bird dog. The hair along the ridge of his spine rose and a low growl started in his throat. Lana searched the landscape and finally saw him: a man crouching behind a thicket of spiny brush. Lana was trapped. The only way out of the area obliged her to walk past the man.

She mustered a commanding voice. "You over there," she called. "Don't move. The dog will attack if you move. I don't control him, and if you move you'll be in serious trouble."

She took a few steps forward. Grizzly, riveted on the man, did not turn to look at her, but as she moved, he moved to keep himself between her and the man, a step sideways, another step, until Lana was safely out of the meadow: then, still holding the man motionless with his intent gaze, he backed off until he had put enough distance between them to turn and trot to Lana's side.

When Lana got back home, she called Ella in Oregon and described what had happened. "Did you train Grizzly to do something like this?" she asked Ella. "How did he know I was in danger?"

"I didn't teach him," Ella told her. "This is the way he is. He knows. He just knows."

"Why didn't he bark or snarl or something?"

"He didn't need to. He knows when to attack and when not to. He didn't need to warn the man because he sensed what the man was up to, and if he decided he needed to attack, he'd have done it with no warning. A dog as intelligent as Grizzly will attack silently and swiftly if he decides he needs to protect you. He's watching over you."

Lana realized this was indeed so because, as much as Grizzly loved to run, he dashed no farther than twenty-five feet in front of her before stopping to look over his shoulder and check on her. He would wait until she caught up to him, then run ahead, stop, check. It was as though there were an invisible circle around Lana, and as soon as Grizzly hit the perimeter, he stopped and waited, sniffing the air, gazing about him, sometimes studying the jagged silhouette of the mountains that walled the flat broad valley where Salt Lake City and the marching suburbs lay, sometimes looking up to the towering clouds sailing like galleons down the valley, sometimes concentrating on an insect scurrying in the dust. Lana often followed the direction of his stare, and through his eyes she began to see the beauty of the natural world and appreciate it. They walked in sun, in rain, in thunderstorms and snow, two wounded creatures on the long road to becoming whole again.

On an afternoon when Tiffy was with them, the three of them were on a hillside when a pack of wild dogs came racing toward them from the low ground, six large dogs running flat out. In an instant Grizzly was off and running to meet the pack, moving as rapidly as they were. Lana shouted but Grizzly did not break stride. "Oh, no," she breathed. "Grizzly, no! They'll kill you!" It was happening so fast that she could do nothing but grab Tiffy's collar and watch.

On Grizzly ran. At top speed, in a move like a karate move, he butted the lead dog, ramming his head into the dog's chest. The dog flew into the air, landed on his side, and lay motionless. As Grizzly turned on the others and hit them, they screamed, high-pitched guttural screams of rage and fear. Grizzly, striking like a rattlesnake, did not snarl or bark, but simply laid about him with bared teeth, powerful haunches, and battering head, felling two more of the dogs before the remaining three, still yelping in fear and rage, ran off with their tails tucked, hindquarters low to the ground. Grizzly surveyed the three dogs he had knocked out, satisfied himself they were no further threat, and trotted back to Lana and Tiffy.

On another outing, Grizzly led Lana on a way they had not gone before and they came to a field where boys in uniforms the color Jeremy had worn were practicing football. A tall boy ran downfield on a pass pattern. The ball sailed over his head, and as he ran to pick it up he pulled off his helmet. His hair was flaxen blond. Grizzly air-scented, broke toward the boy, stopped. Turning, he walked slowly back to Lana, his very bones seeming to sag. Lana dropped to her knees. Grizzly laid his muzzle on her shoulder, her arms went around him, she buried her face in his ruff, and there they huddled, locked in the misery of missing Jeremy.

"Oh, Grizzly," she murmured, "how are we going to get through the rest of our lives?"

As clearly as though he were standing beside her, Jeremy's voice came to her. *Mom, I want you to have Grizzly. Maybe you and he can do something to help other children.*

"Grizzly," Lana said, "maybe it's time we tried. Maybe it's time to find out what we can do together."

Part II

How Much More Is Beginning

5
"Grizzly's Going to Surprise You"

"Dave, I've been thinking," Lana said tentatively that evening. "I've been thinking that I might like to go back to college. There must be kids out there who could use somebody to help them. And maybe, if I can study and read, it would help me too. I have so many questions. How did all this happen? Why did it happen? What does it mean? What is grief all about? Why does it hurt so bad? What makes it better? What makes people tick? What makes some people give themselves so generously and be so loving and supportive, while other people who you think would be there for you turn away?"

"It sounds," said Dave, "as though you want to study psychology."

"I guess I do. Can I?"

"Why not?"

"I don't know if I'm smart enough. I'm not sure I can concentrate."

"You won't know unless you try."

"It's been so long since I was in school. I'm afraid I couldn't do the work."

"I'll help you," Dave said. He had taught writing at the University of Utah before being lured into the corporate world, and he offered to lay out a reading program Lana could follow to ease her back into the habit of studying, a habit that had lapsed twenty years earlier when she married and dropped out of college.

A reading program struck Lana as a good idea and she embarked on the program forthwith, allotting inviolable periods of time to it each day as a first step in reinstituting the discipline of study. At the same time she explored whether the University of Utah would accept her long-ago college credits, and when she found they would, at least in part, she went about applying for admission. In the fall of 1991 she started classes, with the goal of becoming a clinical social worker, a therapist working in the medical arena with sick children.

Occasionally Lana noticed a student walking on campus with a dog and she was envious, for crowds frightened her now and she knew how much more at ease she would feel in a sea of strangers if only Grizzly were beside her. They had grown very close in the year they walked together. An extraordinary degree of communion had developed between them; when Lana despaired or was fearful, Grizzly sensed it and offered his emotional strength for her to draw on.

One of her classes was a three-hour evening class. Explaining to the professor that she intended to use the dog in therapy work and the class would be useful in training him to lie still for long periods, she asked permission to bring Grizzly. What she did not add was that the class was extremely stressful for her because it was a required course in algebra, her weak point, and Grizzly's presence, she felt, might calm and reassure her.

This indeed proved to be so, and not only for her but for her fellow students and the teacher, a man Lana's age who was secure enough, when Grizzly yawned widely and vocally, to admit, "Yeah, Griz, you're right, I'm being boring. Let's move on." For the initial hour of the class, Grizzly was very, very quiet, but he got up and moved around during the second hour, stopping by favorites among the students to have his head petted, and in the third hour he liked to join the professor in front of the class and now and again comment on the lecture with small throaty woofs, which never failed to produce laughter and relieve the tense concentration in the room.

Lana, praising Grizzly for his patience in class, often said on the way home, "Jeremy didn't get to go to college, Griz, so you're going for him." In a way, she felt that was true of herself as well. She came to believe the two of them were on a mission; she would learn to do work that Jeremy, with his instinctive generosity and intuitive sense of how to help people, might well have chosen for himself. With this as incentive, Lana struggled so hard to do well in her classwork that she—who had been so distraught she had scarcely been able to speak a complete sentence when she began this late round of education—made the Dean's list in her second year. This imbued her with the necessary confidence to set her sights on graduate school. Since she would need not only a high grade-point average but a record of volunteer work if she hoped to be one of the few applicants accepted, she contacted an agency that specialized in the psychiatric treatment of children. She was invited to attend an orientation session, and the invitation was expanded to include Grizzly on Lana's assurance that her well-mannered dog would lie perfectly still and that it would save her a fifteen-mile trip home between classes.

Norma Carlson, the coordinator of volunteers at a day treatment center for children, was impressed with Lana's abilities and quickly agreed to have her come on Tuesday and Thursday mornings to be a participant-observer in a treatment group of children with psychiatric problems.

"I have a hunch that Grizzly might be good with disturbed children," Lana remarked, filling in quickly some details of Grizzly's life with Jeremy. She added, "He helped me heal in ways I never thought possible."

Norma Carlson had noted the quiet composure, the dignity, with which Grizzly entered her office, accepted greetings, and settled himself, head on paws, at Lana's side. "There *is* something calming and reassuring about him," she said thoughtfully, sifting pros and cons in her mind.

"Let me come for a couple of weeks to get a feeling for how you work with the kids here," Lana proposed, "and then, if it seems feasible and with your permission, perhaps I can try him in a session."

When she found that a prime tenet of working with the children was never to say no but instead to redirect negative behavior—"Johnny, Susan, why don't we look at this over here?"—she was more certain than ever that Grizzly would be useful. If "this over here" happened to be a large dog instead of an inanimate toy or game, the redirection had every chance of being particularly effective. The children's therapist agreed, and at the start of the third week, with permission, Lana brought Grizzly to the center with her.

When the two of them entered the day treatment room, it was in an uproar thanks to one child, Kevin, who had spun completely out of control. Running, jumping, screaming, he ricocheted off the walls of the room, overturned furniture, kicked the therapist who was trying to restrain him by pinning his arms to his sides, and sent the other children quivering into corners. Even when he was behaving, Kevin was an unappealing boy; he looked and smelled dirty and his nose constantly dripped mucus, which he deliberately smeared over his face. Well aware that people did not like him and did not care to be near him, Kevin reacted violently and often by creating chaos, as he was doing this day.

Lana glanced down at Grizzly. He seemed undisturbed by the tumultuous atmosphere, and as though aware he had a job to do, he set about purposefully greeting each child, offering a paw to be shaken, lowering his head to be petted. The racketing boy forgotten, the children emerged from their corners and settled on mats in a circle around Grizzly and began asking questions: What was the dog's name? What did he like to eat? Where did he live? How many toys did he have? What was his favorite game? When Kevin became aware there was a dog present that had taken attention away from him, his screams died down, and his flailing stopped. Absently he smeared the drizzle from his nose over his cheeks as he stared at Grizzly, settled as majestically as a library lion in the midst of the children. Becoming aware of the stare, Grizzly turned his head. Slowly his tail began to sweep back and forth and he woofled in his throat, his talk sweet and low and sympathetic. Kevin crept closer and closer. Lana watched warily, afraid that this child, himself the victim of abuse, might suddenly strike Grizzly, aiming for his eyes or sensitive nose. But the boy only crept on until finally he laid his head between Grizzly's paws and rested with his arms around Grizzly's neck.

A smile swept over his face. "Grizzly loves me," Kevin announced, his firm tone defying anyone to contradict him. Indeed, it was apparent that it made no difference to Grizzly that Kevin was smeared with mucus and smelled bad. The child needed him and he was there for him.

When the session was over, the therapist raced after Lana. "Did you see? Did you see?" she demanded.

Lana's heart sank. The hour, she thought, had been quiet and ordinary, which meant she must have missed some important observation. "I'm afraid I didn't notice anything," she said apologetically.

"But that's just it!" the therapist exclaimed. "For the first time they behaved like normal kids!"

Grizzly's presence in the group was taken for granted from then on, with the children using him as friend, arbiter, playmate, pillow, and exemplar. Usually it was enough just for him to be there, but there were times when he took it upon himself to play a more active role. This happened one morning when he and Lana arrived to find six of the children sitting on their mats but a seventh, Julie, curled like a snail in a far corner of the room, crying with great, rasping sobs. "We've been trying for an hour to calm her down," the therapist whispered to Lana with a concerned and worried look. "I don't know what else to do except give her some space and let her be."

Grizzly settled as usual in the center of the circle, but his posture was tense, his head uplifted, and he kept turning in Julie's direction. Lana had given him a downstay order, but finally he could stand it no longer. Ignoring Lana, he rose to his feet and slowly headed for the corner where Julie was huddled. When he reached her, he dropped on his stomach and wedged his nose under Julie's elbow to bump her arm away from her face. With his muzzle nudging her chin, he began his woofing talk. Julie went on crying. Grizzly went on crooning. After a while her sobs diminished and she put an arm around his neck, burying her face in his soft ruff. Grizzly sang on. Julie stopped crying. Grizzly woofled encouragingly. Using him as a crutch, Julie struggled to her feet and Grizzly escorted her to the circle. She sat down on her mat. He lay down in the center.

On the basis of such evidence, Lana was more sure than ever that Grizzly had a contribution to make in work with children, and she inquired at an area hospital whether they had a program that brought together kids and animals. She was referred to the child-life specialist, who said, "We have a bunny here, but no official program, no." Lana explained that she had been volunteering with Grizzly at a psychiatric center with such positive results that she would like to volunteer at the hospital as well. "Come ahead. We'd love to have you," the child-life specialist said.

On their first trip to the hospital, Grizzly seemed to understand that he was going to work rather than to class and stepped out enthusiastically, only to be momentarily stymied by the revolving glass door of the hospital. He hesitated, puzzling out how it worked, then led Lana through it. Safely on the other side, he waved his tail and looked quite pleased with himself. Next came a crowded elevator; while Lana assured the occupants they had nothing to fear, Grizzly calmly turned around, faced front, and waited for the doors to open.

Lana began to suspect that in this new situation Grizzly was more poised, more sure of how to behave, than she was. When they started down a high-traffic corridor, he abandoned his customary place on her left and moved over to her right side. Yes, that makes sense, Lana thought; on that side he was between her and the wall and out of the way of oncoming traffic. A further benefit was that they were stopped by fewer people reaching out to pet him; most now contented themselves with saying, "What a handsome dog," as they went by. Grizzly would flick an ear in acknowledgment of the compliment and pace purposefully on.

When they reached the children's wing, children, parents, nurses, and orderlies began appearing in doorways to greet them. Everyone had heard that a dog was coming and were anxious to see him. A mother holding an eighteen-month-old baby asked if the baby could please touch "the beautiful doggie," explaining that they had been away from home a long time and sorely missed their family pet. Squeals from the children and talk and laughter from the parents and nurses created a pleasant uproar in the usually somber hospital corridors as Grizzly passed.

At the child-life office, the director, after being introduced to Grizzly, thanked Lana for coming and assigned a therapist named Paul to accompany them on their rounds and supply Lana with each child's name, diagnosis, length of stay in the hospital, and presumed prognosis. By an unsettling coincidence, the first patient they were to visit, a blond seventeen-year-old with testicular cancer metastatic to the lungs, bore a striking resemblance to Jeremy. Grizzly halted just inside the doorway, ears cocked forward, nose lifted high to scent the air, obviously disconcerted, and Lana wondered if his heart had stopped momentarily, as hers had, at the sight of Steven sitting on the edge of his bed.

Recovering, Grizzly led the way into the room, making chirking sounds of greeting, which the boy acknowledged with solemn politeness. Introductions over, Steven asked, "What does the dog do?"

"He likes to meet people," Lana replied.

"Does he do tricks?"

"Not really."

"Can I make him sit?"

"Well, Griz kind of does his own thing, but you can ask him."

"Here, boy, come and sit beside me." Griz did just that, leaning into Steven's leg so that the two were close as pages in a book. Steven laughed. "Ol' Griz and me are gonna get along just fine," he said, and bent down and laid his cheek against Grizzly's head.

A nurse entered to begin Steven's hookup for chemotherapy. The look that came into the boy's eyes was chillingly familiar to

Lana, but she fancied that it was perhaps just a touch less despairing than it would otherwise have been because Grizzly was there by his side, not moving even when an IV tube carrying water to hydrate the young man came loose and the contents sprayed over Grizzly's coat. When the hookup was complete and the nurse had left, Grizzly took it into his head to act silly. He fell on the floor, crooning and waving his legs in the air, not stopping until he made Steven laugh.

On their way to the second room, Paul briefed Lana on the nine-year-old they were going to see. A kidney transplant patient, he was deeply depressed, sure he would never be well again. Tubes and machines crowded the room. The boy's weary mother was slumped in the only chair, and the boy himself lay in bed, whimpering in pain. Grizzly was quiet and slow, deliberate in his movements, careful not to brush against a tube or knock over a stand as he and Lana approached the bed. He thrust up his big head and the boy, patting blindly, found his nose, touched it, and, smiling, opened his eyes. A bell went off on one of the machines, and Lana, recognizing it as a signal for them to get out of the way, told the boy that Grizzly would be back to see him first thing the next week.

At the door of the third room, the mother of the patient, with a worn and frightened look Lana knew all too well, greeted them and said her daughter Melody, who was eleven, had only within the past twenty-four hours regained consciousness. The little form on the bed was swathed in plaster except for the bruised head and a large, bloody wound on one thigh. Despite the clear plastic bandage over the wound, Grizzly smelled the blood and carefully walked nearer to inspect the site from a distance. Satisfied that the cut was being cared for, he relaxed and put his head under the fingers stretched out to feel for him.

Lana explained to Melody that Grizzly had been concerned about the wound until he saw that the doctors had stitched it up. "I got hurt pretty bad," Melody said. "I was riding my bike and a car hit me." Melody's mother explained that the girl had broken her pelvis, both arms, and both legs and had cut an artery in her leg. "I'm awful tired," Melody said, "but I'd love to see Grizzly. Mom, could you lower the bed?"

Even with the bed lowered, it was not going to be possible for Melody to get a real look at Grizzly unless he stood up on his hind legs, and since he had been taught not to jump up on anyone, he never did that. There was just one exception. Back in the days when they were in Oregon and he went to stay with Ella, he reared up on his hind legs to greet her with a kiss. Would he do it for Lana?

"Up, Griz," Lana said, patting her chest.

Grizzly cocked his head to one side as if to say, Really?

"Yes, Griz, it's okay. Come ahead. Up, Griz."

Grizzly took a deep breath, braced himself, and reared up, all ninety-five pounds of him, slamming his paws down on Lana's shoulders. She was five-feet-two, and with Grizzly standing on his hind legs, his head was almost level with hers. He gave Lana a kiss and stood there as long as he could manage it while Melody exclaimed over how large and beautiful he was.

"I've fallen in love," she declared. "Please, I want to touch him again before you go." Grizzly dropped down on all fours, thrust his muzzle under Melody's fingers, and sang a small song.

The last room Lana and Grizzly visited that day was dark and silent: no lights, no TV, no radio. Paul knocked and said, "Bennett, is it okay if Grizzly comes in for a visit? He's a German shepherd and very friendly."

"Yeah," the boy answered with barely a hint of life in his voice. He was an extremely thin, lethargic, depressed sixteen-year-old with cystic fibrosis whose prognosis was poor. "I've been waiting all morning to see him. Come here, Grizzly."

Immediately Grizzly left Lana's side and trotted to the bed, ignoring the oxygen tube and the swishing sound of a respirator. The boy struggled to a sitting position on the side of the bed and hugged Grizzly as though he were his own dog. A moment later he was down on the floor, tickling Grizzly's stomach and laughing as the dog's hind leg scratched imaginary itches in the air. Grizzly nibbled at a forepaw and crooned, behavior Lana had never seen before, which was clearly intended to amuse and cheer the sick boy. When it was time for Grizzly to go, the boy buried his head in Grizzly's ruff and hugged him as though he knew he would never see him again. Indeed, when next Lana and Grizzly visited, there was someone else in the room. The boy had died.

Grizzly's effect on patients was so positive, so marked, that Lana began to wonder if there were other people taking animals into treatment situations and having the same experience. She resolved to research the question at the library, but before she found time to do that, Dave came home from work with news that a colleague of his named Grace Whitaker, who owned two Labradors and belonged to a dog club in her hometown of Provo, had told him that a woman was coming to Salt Lake City on Saturday of that week to talk about therapy dogs. Lana arrived early to claim a front-row seat, but her enthusiasm leaked away as the woman described visits to nursing homes with dogs who wore funny costumes and jumped through hoops. Even if that had been the sort of endeavor that interested Lana, Grizzly was too proud and dignified a dog to do any such thing.

At the end of the talk, Lana lingered to thank the woman and say how cheerful it must be for patients in nursing homes to be entertained in this way. But, she added, she had in mind something designed to help in the treatment of patients. Did the woman know of anyone doing that sort of work?

"Call Ernie Moss," the woman said. "She raises Dobermans and is president of the Humane Society in Ogden. She will know."

Ernie Moss's first remark to Lana was, "You need to get your dog tested to see if he is capable of doing therapy work." Lana told her about Grizzly's having been raised by a sick boy, about their volunteering to work with children at the psychiatric facility and the hospital, and about the fact that Grizzly was proving better qualified to teach her how to do animal-assisted therapy than she was to instruct him. Moss admitted that Grizzly sounded qualified and agreed to send Lana an application for membership in an organization to which she belonged that promoted animal-assisted therapy. An advantage of the organization, she gave Lana to understand, was the availability of liability insurance to cover any injury caused by the dog, and since that seemed a wise idea, Lana filled out the application forms for membership and sent them in. In return, she received a dog tag to hang around Grizzly's neck that announced I AM A THERAPY DOG.

"I guess that makes us legitimate, Griz," Lana said, and she used it on visits to the hospital. No insurance forms came, however, and when she inquired, she learned that the hospital or nursing home had to obtain the insurance, not the individual. Since no hospital or clinic official had mentioned liability, Lana decided to forget about it. The newsletters of the organization seemed equally unhelpful. Amateurish and poorly written, they dealt only with amusing capers visiting animals could perform. Nothing in them provided useful guidance to Lana as she and Grizzly continued their volunteer work.

The two of them arrived at the hospital one day just after a nine-year-old boy had been admitted. Like Bennett, Christopher suffered from cystic fibrosis and had been coming into the hospital at intervals throughout his short life. Familiarity with hospital procedures had not made him any less frightened and unhappy at having to undergo them. When Lana knocked on the door of his room and looked in, she saw that a tearful Christopher was squirming as a nurse tried to get an IV needle in his arm.

"Would you like to meet Grizzly?" Lana asked from the doorway. Christopher's head swiveled, his eyes widened, and his jaw dropped as the tears dried on his face; in all his times in the hospital, he had never been visited by a dog before. Grizzly strolled to his side and hum-grunted a greeting.

"Wow! Can I pet him?" the boy said.

"Sure, as soon as the nurse says it's okay."

"Hurry," Christopher urged the nurse, thrusting his arm out and holding it steady. "Hurry up so I can pet the dog." With the patient so suddenly cooperative, it was only a moment before the IV was running. Christopher slid to the floor and stroked Grizzly's head, at first tentatively, somewhat awed by the size of the dog, and then more confidently as Grizzly woofled encouragement.

Suddenly the woofing stopped and Grizzly turned toward the doorway with a chilling stare. Through the door came a technician with a tray bearing vials of blood. Grizzly had smelled the blood, and his fixed glare said, *Oh, no, you don't. You're not coming in here*. The message was explicit enough to stop the technician in her tracks.

"Grizzly," Lana said, patting his back soothingly, "it's okay." His stare swerved to her. "It's okay. She's not going to hurt Christopher."

Grizzly's body relaxed, as if to say, *All right, then, if you say it's okay*, and he subsided beside Christopher, who was crowing with delight over Grizzly's clear intention to defend him from harm.

"Are you sure you've got that dog under control?" the technician asked apprehensively, reluctant to advance even when Lana nodded and smiled her most confident, reassuring smile.

So caught up was Christopher in the pleasure of Grizzly's company that he made no fuss about the drawing of his blood, and neither did Grizzly, who was resting beside the boy. Again, all Christopher wanted was for the technician to be finished and gone. The minute she was, he asked Lana eagerly, "Could I go for a walk with Grizzly?"

Lana, gesturing to the IV pole, was about to say no when she had a sudden memory. "My son was able to go for walks with his IV if I wheeled it along behind him. Maybe the nurse could wheel the pole and you and I could walk beside Grizzly."

"That would work," said the nurse.

But now it was Christopher who was fearful. "Will Grizzly pull me? Will he make me fall down? Because if I fall down . . ."

The nurse answered when Lana, realizing she would be taking a risk, hesitated. "The dog'll be fine," the nurse said with perfect confidence even though her acquaintance with Grizzly was only minutes long.

With Christopher clasping Grizzly's pistol-grip leash, Lana on Grizzly's other side, and the nurse in back wheeling the IV pole, the procession started down the hallway. Quickly Grizzly moved out several paces in front of them. Oh, dear, Lana thought, how will he know where to go? Aloud she said, "If you want Grizzly to go slower or to turn, Christopher, just ask him." And again she thought, That was stupid, Lana. Grizzly doesn't know left from right. I'll have to tug on the leash.

Christopher ordered loud and clear, "Turn left, Grizzly."

One of Grizzly's ears swiveled back and, without further ado, he turned left. Christopher chortled with delight that the massive dog had obeyed his command, and Lana silently applauded the coincidence that Grizzly had happened to turn the correct way.

They came to another intersection of corridors, with three directions available: left, right, and straight ahead. "Grizzly, uh . . . turn right," Christopher said. Grizzly turned right. "Grizzly, stop," the boy said. Grizzly stopped. "Grizzly, go." Grizzly moved forward. And so it went, Christopher giving orders, Grizzly obeying them. When they had made a full circle of the wing and Christopher was back in his room again, the boy was laughing and happy, no longer frightened and miserable. The visit with Grizzly had changed his day, perhaps his whole hospital stay.

Arriving home, Lana threw her pocketbook down on the couch and reached for the phone to call Klamath Falls. "Ella, what is it with this dog? I don't understand how he could have known what the little boy was asking him to do. He's never heard those commands before. Unless you taught him?"

"Not I."

"How does he know left from right?"

"He just knows."

"You didn't teach him? You didn't train him?"

"Absolutely not. I said from the beginning that he was a special dog."

"I thought you meant he'd just be special for Jeremy. What else does he know that I don't know about?"

Ella's warm chuckle came over the line. "You just keep watching him. Grizzly's going to surprise you."

6
The Good Shepherd Association

Talk of Grizzly spread through the hospital, and when Lana and Grizzly arrived for their volunteer stint the following week, a nurse came running down the hallway to intercept them. "Oh, please," she said, "I'm from the oncology unit and I've got a patient who's been here fifty-two days. The doctors can't find what's wrong with him. They've tried everything, and they haven't a clue. He's so discouraged and depressed. Please, could you bring the dog? The boy grew up with animals on a ranch and he's just eighteen. . . ." The nurse's voice trailed off but her face continued to plead.

Lana had to refuse. "The child-life therapist has a schedule of patients who are looking forward to a visit from the dog today. I can't disappoint them, and an hour is about the dog's limit." Lana was as sensitive to Grizzly as he was to the children and she knew the work was exhausting for him. He absorbed the emotions of the children directly, emotions that were not mediated by words but came in through his senses. He held himself open to them, and by the end of an hour she knew he had had about all he could take. But the appeal in the nurse's face was so stark, so urgent, that

Lana softened her refusal. "After we do the visits here, if Griz is not too tired. . . ."

"Please," said the nurse once more. "I'll come back in an hour."

When the rounds of the children's rooms were over, Lana checked her watch and her schedule. It was not just Grizzly she had to think about but her own needs. She was taking fourteen credit hours at the university and she had begun teaching piano again in order to earn money to pay for her courses, which meant that she had to shuttle back and forth between the campus and home. Her grand piano, retrieved from its stay in storage in Seattle, was at the house and her pupils came to her there.

The nurse from the oncology unit reappeared, concern for her patient still etched on her face. "Lead the way," Lana said, pocketing the small notebook in which she kept track of her appointments. "I've got a free hour and Grizzly's had an easy time so far."

As they moved through the corridors and rode the elevator, the nurse described the strange illness ravaging the eighteen-year-old, wasting his muscles and affecting his vision and speech. A snapshot taped on the door of his room showed a strong, tanned young man dressed in blue jeans, plaid shirt, and cowboy hat leaning against the fence of a corral, a hound dog at his feet and one hand negligently flung on the neck of a horse looking over the fence.

"He looks like the kid brother in a John Wayne movie," Lana whispered.

The nurse shook her head sadly. "Once. No more. We put the picture here to remind us to treat him like he was, not like he is now." She knocked lightly on the door and led the way in. "Richard, you have some visitors."

The snapshot bore no resemblance to the wasted figure who lay in the bed, plastic tubes like downed power lines tethering him to IV poles. Lana was thrown back to memories of Jeremy fading away from her as surely and inexorably as this young man was being lost to the people who loved him. Grizzly air-scented, checking that this was not the ghost of his boy. He looked up at Lana, and when she nodded, he led her forward, skirting the side of the bed, and silently laid his head near the young man's shoulder.

Feeling the pressure on the bed, Richard slid a wasted, contracted arm across his body and patted the place to determine what it was. His hand encountered Grizzly. He dragged his eyes open. "Hey, the wolves are closing in."

Lana smiled. "My name's Lana and this is Grizzly Ridge. He's come to say hello to you."

"Gee, where did you get such a gorgeous dog? He's terrific!"

"Well, he just sort of came along."

"I have a dog who just sort of came along, but his genes are a sight more mixed up than this one's." They both grinned and the conversation swung along from there, the two people trading anecdotes about dogs while Grizzly stood quietly by the bed with Richard's hand resting on his head. Lana explained how Grizzly routinely would come looking for her after he had eaten his breakfast or dinner, and, if she was behind a closed door, would bark until she opened it. She would listen to his *Munk, munk,* which meant *Thank you,* and say, in return, "You're welcome, Griz," and then, satisfied, he would go away.

"What a great dog," Richard said. "I wish I could get a better look at him. Do you suppose he could get up on a chair?"

"He's never done that and he's awfully big." Lana was dubious but then she remembered what Ella had said and spoke resolutely. "If it's the right thing to do, Griz will do it." She pulled a straight chair close to the bed. "Griz, do you think you can get up on the chair?"

Griz heard the question in her voice and understood the chair was for him. Cautiously he placed his front paws on it, bobbed through a few sample dips, and jumped. He teetered, had to catch himself by putting a paw on the bed, but then tucked his tail, turned around, and lowered his hindquarters onto the chair. Richard exclaimed again over his handsomeness, and as he and Lana chatted, he let his fingers rummage in the comforting feel of the dog's fur. They talked, not of illness and hospitals, but of open acres and horses and mountains and trails, the rewarding, balanced, equable world of the out-of-doors. Grizzly was quiet and patient, he and Lana giving the young man back for a brief time his identity as a person.

"When can I see Grizzly again?" Richard asked when a half hour had gone by and Lana thought Grizzly must certainly be tired and uncomfortable although he had given no sign of it.

Lana told him their scheduled times in the hospital and promised she and Grizzly would look in on him. "I won't forget," she said. "But if I do, Grizzly will remind me."

It happened that on their next visit Richard was about to be wheeled to a physical therapy session, and he begged for Grizzly and Lana to accompany him. Grizzly led the way, responding to Richard's directions. When they arrived at the therapy room, he paid serious attention as a strong young woman massaged one of Richard's legs with probing, digging, kneading fingers and then several times bent it double at the knee and stretched it out again. "Now you do it," she instructed, and Richard, although it obviously caused him pain, complied. When he faltered, Grizzly woofed, urging him on. Amused, Richard accused Grizzly of being a nag, but he tried again. In such fashion, did he work through the prescribed number of exercises, and the therapist pronounced herself satisfied. She held out her hand to Grizzly, who gravely placed his paw in it, and thanked the dog for being such an effective motivator.

Four more times Lana and Grizzly visited Richard. His vision worsened to the point where he could no longer see, but he chuckled when Grizzly clacked his teeth and took comfort from the feel of the massive head when Grizzly worked his muzzle under Richard's hand. The last time they returned, the snapshot of the life-filled young man with his dog and horse was gone and another name was on the card slotted in beside the door. Lana looked down at Grizzly. His tail was at half mast. He knew without her telling him that Richard, like Jeremy, was gone.

They walked in silence down the corridor. Coming toward them was a middle-aged couple, the tearful wife shuffling along in slippers, holding her heavily bandaged hand at an awkward angle, while the husband, with desperate whispers, was clearly trying to comfort her. From the truncated shape of the bandages, Lana guessed that the woman's fingers had been amputated. The couple was moving along so unseeingly that she stopped with Grizzly to let them pass. Suddenly the man said, "Look, honey," and swung his wife a bit to see Grizzly. "We have a German shepherd at home," he told Lana. "A female. Our son's taking care of her. We miss her so much."

"So much," his wife echoed.

"It's hard being away from home, isn't it," Lana said. They talked for a few more minutes while the man stroked Grizzly's head and his wife commented on how big, how gentle, how well-behaved Grizzly was. By the time Lana and Grizzly moved on, the woman was smiling. Having something outside herself to focus on had stopped her tears.

Lana saw the same thing happen again a few minutes later with another woman whom tragedy had struck. A nurse stopped Lana in the corridor to ask her to bring Grizzly to a nearby room. "Perhaps you saw the story in the newspaper," the nurse said as she led the way. "Mrs. Feliciano and her husband had a candy store. They were held up, and the gunmen killed her husband and badly wounded her. She and her husband were together so long that she can't imagine her life without him. She believes she has no life anymore. I'm hoping the dog will let her think of something else for a few moments."

The nurse entered the room first. "I've brought someone to see you, Mrs. Feliciano," she said cheerily.

The tiny woman in the bed slowly turned her head on the pillow. Her face froze in shock, her eyes opened wide. Clearly, the last thing she had anticipated coming through the door was a dog who, at ninety-five pounds, almost certainly weighed more than she did. Lana led Grizzly to the side of the bed, and he gave the hand lying on the counterpane a nudge and a muzzle kiss. For something to say, Lana remarked that because he had been making rounds in the hospital, Grizzly was probably hungry, and if she liked, Mrs. Feliciano could give him a dog biscuit. A bit apprehensively, Mrs. Feliciano took the biscuit from Lana and held it out to Grizzly. His mouth opened wide and Mrs. Feliciano drew her hand back hastily. Grizzly waited until she summoned the courage to bring the biscuit forward again. Daintly he plucked it from her fingers.

Mrs. Feliciano smiled in relief. "Oh, my, I was afraid he was going to take my whole hand, but he's really very polite, isn't he?"

Grizzly snapped his teeth. "He's agreeing with you," Lana told her. "Griz, would you like to speak for Mrs. Feliciano?"

Grizzly instead held out his paw. Mrs. Feliciano accepted it as though it were the hand of a gentleman. "Thank you for coming to see me, Grizzly," she said. Grizzly woofled in his throat. "You *can* talk!" she exclaimed.

I can when I want to, his high-and-mighty tail conveyed with a swish as he left the room.

The nurse closed the door behind them. "It's the first time I've seen Mrs. Feliciano show any animation. I think she may turn the corner now." She was thanking Lana when a man moving in an aura of authority stalked past them, everything about him stiff with importance, from his gray hair moving in iron waves across his scalp, to his starched white jacket with three gray-capped pens clipped in an exact line in his breast pocket. He nodded crisply at the nurse and narrowed his gray eyes behind steel-rimmed glasses to take in Lana and Grizzly. It was so unusual for someone to pass Grizzly by without smiling that Lana asked in a whisper who he was and was told that he was one of the bigwigs in the hospital.

That night, at home, Lana received a telephone call from the director of the children's unit. "What were you doing in the oncology wing without permission? The big boss saw you there, and he doesn't approve of animals in hospitals. You broke the rules by going off the children's floor."

Lana rallied to defend herself. "I'm sorry you're upset, but I was asked to go there by a staff member who went along with me. I had no idea I was doing anything wrong. I'm a volunteer, not an employee, and you can't expect volunteers not to break rules they know nothing about." She suggested they make an appointment to talk about this and some other problems that had been on her mind.

When she and the director were face-to-face, the first question Lana asked was whether the staff was happy with the work she and Grizzly were doing.

"Yes, everyone here loves you and Grizzly."

"Then if you want us to continue, I would like to have some written guidelines on policy so that I don't cause problems for anyone. I want to know what I can and cannot do."

"I'm too busy this week. You'll have to wait until I have time."

"Then I think a child-life therapist should be with me at all times to make sure Grizzly and I are behaving in safe and appropriate ways."

"We're too busy for that. I don't have enough staff as it is."

"Then what about having training sessions for volunteers? Reprimands after the fact are not a very good way to treat people who are giving their time and making the effort to be here."

Lana received her answer via a letter that arrived two days later, the gist of which was that she was asking too much of staff, that the hospital was unwilling and unable at the present time to provide her with the assistance she was requesting, and that, in the opinion of the hospital, "This work is inappropriate for you."

This high-handed verdict cut the ground from under Lana's confidence. Crushed by it, Lana accused herself of being inadequate, inept, stupid, a horrible person.

"It's the tone of the letter that's horrible, not you," Dave assured her repeatedly in the following days as Lana wrestled with the conviction that from now on she would be blackballed by the medical community if she and Grizzly tried to work with sick children. When finally she struggled through to a place from which she could view the incident a bit more dispassionately, she realized that the people involved at the hospital had not understood her concept of bringing Grizzly, not only to be petted, but also so that she might observe the effect of an animal on hospitalized patients. She had not communicated her belief that animal and handler could function as part of the treatment team. Failing to explain that she was a volunteer with a purpose had occasioned her being looked down on as just a woman with time on her hands and a dog she liked to show off. Lana told herself that, having worked in hospitals before, she should have known how to play the political game, to take account of the hierarchy and go through the proper channels. As it was, she mourned, she had ruined her chance to demonstrate that animal-assisted therapy was a valid paraprofession waiting to be born.

At least now she had time to spend in the university library researching the topic of animals and people in therapeutic settings. Predictably, she found articles about animals being taken to visit patients in nursing homes, anecdotal reports about the pleasure this seemed to give the patients, and a few scientific studies detailing a specific therapeutic effect of pets in lowering blood pressure and heart rates. There was also a study demonstrating that patients who owned pets had a better recovery rate from illness than a control group of patients without pets. Lana could corroborate this from her own experience the night before Jeremy died when Grizzly's warm presence had eased her stomach pains; even now, when she felt stressed or in pain, she found that reaching out to stroke Grizzly made her feel better. But it did not seem to her that the easing of pain could only be accomplished by the patient's own pet. She had the evidence of having been on the children's floor in the hospital one day when Christopher, the nine-year-old with cystic fibrosis, was being wheeled to his room from the recovery room after surgery and the boy caught sight of Grizzly in the corridor.

"No, no," one of the nurses said. "You can't have Grizzly come see you now. You need to be quiet and rest. You have to be careful of your stitches."

"Oh, please! I want to see Grizzly. Please! *Please!*"

The boy's parents, knowing his fondness for the big dog, added their voices to Christopher's, and Grizzly was allowed in the room while Christopher was being settled in bed. Then Christopher asked if Grizzly could come up on his bed. At the parents' urging, a clean drawsheet was put in place, pillows were lined up along the boy's side, and Grizzly was directed to put his front paws on the bed. Lana slowly lifted his hindquarters and placed him full-length beside Christopher, keeping her hands on his body to remind him to remain perfectly still. Christopher talked to Grizzly and played with Grizzly's ears, indifferent to the misery of the lengthy abdominal incision that a few minutes earlier had had him moaning and his parents pale with anxiety. Now there was laughter in the room, color in cheeks, peace in faces.

But, barred from the hospital, Lana had no way of demonstrating the correctness of her hypothesis concerning animal-assisted therapy. At the start of her junior year at the university, she elected to take a course in community psychology, and two or three weeks into the course she found that one of the requirements was to invent a nonprofit organization to undertake a community service project involving people serving others in need of help. In a meeting with the professor, Lana outlined her idea for animal-assisted therapy.

The professor objected that he was asking for new ideas, for projects that had not been done before. "People are already taking animals into nursing homes."

"Yes, but that's not what I want to do," Lana told him. "I want to go to kids who have cancer or cystic fibrosis or some other life-threatening illness that keeps them in the hospital for long periods. I want to train people to take their animals, who will also be trained, to do therapy, not just visits where the animals wear funny hats and give kisses. I envision animal-assisted therapy to be an auxiliary treatment, like physical therapy or occupational therapy, art or music therapy, carried out by trained, licensed paraprofessionals."

"Animals doing therapy? I very much doubt that's a viable notion, Mrs. Davis. But go ahead and draft a proposal, and I'll tell you whether it seems worth my time and yours."

Lana did so, but when she took the written proposal to the professor, he still expressed doubt. "I'd come up with an alternate idea if I were you," he said. "In the meantime, put together an oral presentation for the class and see what kind of reaction you get."

Lana consulted Dave, who suggested that, since people like to hear stories about other people, she tell the class about how Grizzly's consumption of tomatoes, pickles, and a slice of onion enticed a patient into eating, how he twice distracted the boy with cystic fibrosis from the pain of his illness, how he had lifted Richard from the bog of depression and been an encouraging companion in his last days. Lana accepted Dave's advice and decided to describe these visits, as well as a visit she and Grizzly had made to a young boy whose hands and feet had been blown off in an accident with a hand grenade. The boy was about to go into surgery and he had, he admitted to Lana, "a bad case of the scaries."

"You know," Lana told him, "you don't have to be there in the operating room while the doctors are working to fix you up. If you want to, you can go walking in fields and woods with Grizzly instead. Shall I tell you how?" The wide-eyed little boy nodded wonderingly. "All right. Close your eyes. Now, imagine that you and Grizzly have stepped out on the porch of a log cabin where you have had a delicious night's sleep in a feather bed and a good big breakfast of your favorite things to eat."

"Bananas," said the boy.

"Bananas. On cereal?"

"Cornflakes."

"Right, a bowl of cornflakes and sliced bananas and cold milk, and Grizzly has had two big dog biscuits and the milk in the bottom of your cereal bowl—"

The boy chuckled. "My mother wouldn't like him eating out of my bowl."

"Ah, but this is your cabin and you can do anything you like in it. You and Grizzly are about to take a walk. The sun is shining on the meadow of tall grass that stretches out in front of the cabin. The field is all coppery and golden, with a narrow path just wide enough for you and Grizzly to walk together. You start down it. The grasses brush against your legs and the sun is warm on your back. Listen. Is there a bird singing?"

"It's in a tree at the edge of the meadow."

"And there's another up ahead, a tiny goldfinch balancing on a stalk of milkweed, swaying in the breeze. When you and Grizzly come near, it flies ahead as though it's leading you."

"Into the forest."

"Into a peaceful forest with a carpet of pine needles and squirrels playing tag in the trees. . . ."

"And tigers."

"Friendly tigers as small as cats, who purr and rub back and forth against your legs."

"And tickle."

"And tickle, and tell you that sometimes they, too, have the scaries, but not in the meadow with the blue wildflowers and not in the friendly forest with the brook and the waterfall and the cave—"

The boy interrupted excitedly. "Is there a cave?"

"There is."

"Can I go there?"

"With Grizzly. Let Grizzly lead you there."

"Grizzly won't let anything bad happen to me."

"Whenever you think anything bad might be going to happen, go with Grizzly to the cave, where it's safe and warm. He'll look after you."

Two orderlies, coming to wheel the boy to the operating room, appeared in the doorway. The boy thanked Lana for bringing Grizzly to see him and assured Lana that walking with Grizzly was a great way to get rid of the scaries.

Her presentation to the class would be most persuasive, Lana decided, if Grizzly was present when she delivered it, particularly since the class was one that she had not hitherto taken Grizzly to. Predictably, there were admiring exclamations when the large, handsome dog took his place beside her in front of the class. Lana said, "Griz, take it," and put a dog biscuit between her teeth. She crouched to Grizzly's level and he cocked his head, drew his mouth back over his teeth, and extracted the biscuit as delicately as a bumblebee drawing nectar from a flower, not touching Lana by so much as a whisker.

"It delights a child when he takes a biscuit like this," Lana told the class. "The child feels empowered when he or she orders this large creature to take a biscuit or fetch a ball or go for a walk and turn left or right and the dog does it willingly, happily. Sick children have so little they can control in their lives that it makes them feel special when the dog obeys them and talks to them. Yes, talks to them," Lana said in answer to the skeptical looks. She knelt and put her arms around Grizzly's neck, and Grizzly laid his muzzle on her shoulder and obligingly crooned in her ear. The students appeared to be impressed, and they were touched by Lana's description of his unusual cooperation in the effort to get Shelley to eat.

"But," said one when she told of Grizzly's curing "the scaries," "that's you leading the child in a visualization exercise. The dog didn't do anything."

"True," Lana answered, "but what do you suppose the child's reaction would have been to a middle-aged woman showing up in his hospital room and saying, "'Come take a walk in a meadow with me'"?

"He would have yelled for someone to get the crazy lady out of his room."

"Exactly," Lana said. "Animals interest children—almost everyone, for that matter. Their presence breaks the ice, bridges the gap between adult and child. They are a living creature for a child to touch and pet and get down on the floor with and hug. Also, children are used to stories about animals, so they almost always go right along with any suggestion of what they can imagine doing with an animal companion. When it's adults you're dealing with, a dog can take them out of themselves, remind them of happier times, bring a touch of normalcy into an abnormal and distressing situation."

"Isn't Grizzly a somewhat special dog?"

"A very special dog," Lana agreed. "He has a great sixth sense. He's taught me how to approach people, how to handle situations. What I want to do is teach other people what he has taught me and work out ways for their animals to become therapy dogs—not just visiting pets but animals doing therapy."

"What institutions are going to allow animals to be brought in?"

"What about dogs carrying disease?"

"How about using cats too?"

The questions flew as the class debated Lana's proposal. One student, much in favor of it, described how her exceedingly ill mother had turned her face toward recovery when her beloved cat was smuggled into the hospital for a visit, and another spoke of how his dog had cheered him through a bout of rheumatic fever as a child. The class came to a consensus that the project was worth exploring. But then one last question came up. "What will you call it? Your hypothetical organization has to have a name."

As usual when she was at a loss about something that concerned Grizzly, Lana called Klamath Falls.

"Is Grizzly sort of the inspiration for this class project?" Ella asked.

"Absolutely."

"Then you could call it The Good Shepherd, because that's what Grizzly is."

"Um. Or maybe The Good Shepherd Association because the idea is to involve other volunteers and their dogs."

"Sounds good to me," Ella said.

"The Good Shepherd Association. Yes, I like it. That's what I'll call it. You're like Grizzly, Ella. I can always count on you to come up with the right thing."

7
Sight and Insight

The class assignment specifically was to invent and describe "a nonprofit resource to serve the community." It was not intended that the students carry out the projects, merely provide a rationale for the service they were proposing, an outline of the steps that would need to be followed in establishing such a service, and a description of how the service could be presumed to operate and the benefit it would theoretically be to the community.

Lana set all these postulates concerning her proposal down on paper and asked Dave to review the result, which he was more than qualified to do because he possessed a master's degree in social work, had twelve years of experience in the field, and had once been assistant director of a social service agency. His reaction was blunt: "Lana, I don't think your plan has much chance of succeeding. The concept is too vague, and because of the way it's written, it seems to hinge on the exceptional abilities of one dog."

"I'm sure other dogs could be trained to do what Grizzly does."

"Then you'll have to describe how you'd train them, along with how you'd pick out likely dogs in the first place, how you'd find and train the volunteers. . . . Here, I'll make a list of the topics that ought to be covered."

As she reorganized and reworked her paper according to Dave's list, Lana kept wondering if her plan really did bear any relation to reality. Would someone who worked with animals be able to devise ways to train dogs to do the types of things Grizzly did intuitively? She longed to talk to an experienced trainer of dogs, and when she took Grizzly to the veterinarian to have his shots updated, she asked if he happened to know of anyone.

"You could call Paulette Bethel," he suggested. "She has a Doberman named Onyx that she has trained for Schutzhund and AKC competition."

Lana knew that AKC stood for the American Kennel Club, which meant that Paulette Bethel would know how to train a dog for show, and she assumed that Schutzhund signified obedience; both together suggested that Paulette Bethel was someone who could give her an opinion about whether what she was proposing was feasible. Lana telephoned her, and finding that the pleasant-sounding Paulette, like everyone else, thought she was talking about pet visits, asked if they might meet. Paulette remarked that she frequently joined five other women for lunch on the day they took their dogs to visit nursing homes and suggested that Lana might like to come along. Perfect, thought Lana. Here are six women already volunteering with their dogs; if they're interested in what I want to do, it will be a good sign.

But they were not. Their reaction was that trying to use dogs as part of a treatment team was sort of a nutsy idea. Anyway, they said, what's the matter with what we're doing? Nursing homes liked them to visit, the dogs seemed to enjoy it, and volunteering a couple of hours a week was a different proposition from going in for all sorts of training. Only Paulette Bethel listened thoughtfully and seemed somewhat intrigued, and Cheryl Weaver, a veterinary technician and the owner of a Rottweiler named Megan, did not flat out say no as the others did. When her class paper detailing how she envisioned the project was finished, Lana gave Paulette and Cheryl a copy to read, at their request.

Their reaction took Lana by surprise. "Let's do it," Paulette said calmly.

"Actually do it?" Lana said.

"Why not? I've trained dogs and horses and Cheryl has worked with a variety of animals, so we know a fair amount about animal behavior, and you're already convinced from your own experience that animal-assisted therapy is valuable."

"It is, I'm sure of it."

"So let's do it," Cheryl echoed.

"Well, all right. Yes. Sure. Hey, that's great!" Lana was so pleased she was almost stuttering as they settled around a table to begin a series of meetings on the practical matters of how and where and when.

In her paper Lana had modeled The Good Shepherd Association after nonprofit human-services organizations, and the three of them decided to stick to that pattern but with some of the characteristics of dog clubs added, such as holding monthly meetings to which handlers brought their dogs and where training routines were run through, advice given, training mistakes corrected, and grooming tips dispensed. They discussed at length the things volunteers would need to know and the attributes dogs would have to have, and they began writing out policy and procedure guidelines. At one meeting, Cheryl Weaver remarked that she had seen a notice in the veterinary office where she worked about an organization called the Delta Society that encouraged therapeutic use of the "human-animal" bond. It had been started by a doctor and was based in Renton, Washington. Lana called the society and asked for information. From the material sent, it appeared that the Delta Society, as well as promoting pet visits, was also going in the direction of animal-assisted therapy and was developing standards to be met by handlers and their dogs. Seminars for pet handlers were offered at which attendees could earn certification as trained evaluators of animals and instructors of volunteers. Lana, Paulette, and Cheryl decided the certification would give their fledgling organization the stamp of legitimacy, and the three of them, plus Grace Whitaker, the colleague of Dave's who owned two chocolate-colored Labradors, flew to Seattle to take the training.

Lana found the seminar unimpressive, for at this early stage in the Delta Society's history, animal-assisted therapy (AAT) was barely a dot on the horizon. Its time was coming as people like Lana realized the possibilities and made beginning efforts, and in a few short years the Delta Society would be offering in-depth information and training programs, but at this point what Lana and her colleagues were given was essentially eight hours of training in very basic animal-assisted activity visits. This was a little disappointing, but Lana did become aware of how much she had yet to learn and that the Delta Society was a valuable means for keeping up with the latest research and for contact with experienced handlers in the field. It put her in touch with a network of professionals—in particular with Program Director Maureen Fredrickson, who spent many hours mentoring her by telephone in animal-assisted therapy.

To Lana's way of thinking, the standards proposed by the Delta Society for volunteer selection, animal training, cleanliness guidelines, and so on were not rigorous enough for the type of population she wanted to serve. She set to work elaborating her own program of training for new volunteers, while Paulette, after closely observing Grizzly at work, undertook to fashion a training regimen for handlers to follow in teaching their animals the necessary skills to function in therapy situations.

Lana was still volunteering at the psychiatric clinic for children, and Paulette, going along with her to observe, saw that a therapy dog had to learn to feel comfortable about having children rest against him, pull his ears and tail, feel him all over, and pry his mouth open to look at his teeth. He needed to be patient and accepting, good-humored, willing to play if asked to retrieve a ball but content to lie still when that was indicated. He had to learn to take a biscuit without snapping at it and to accept being combed and brushed by the children. He also had to learn to be walked by children without pulling on the leash and to respond promptly to basic commands like *sit, stay, down, forward, stop, left, right, wait, take it,* and *easy.*

"But how is any dog going to be trained to do that?" Paulette said to Lana one morning, in mock despair, after watching Grizzly pull off one of his amazing feats. They had taken him to a school for deaf and blind children where they were discussing the possibility of Good Shepherd volunteers working at the school. They were standing in one of the classrooms talking with a teacher, who mentioned that she was particularly concerned about an eight-year-old named Tyler who had been successfully treated for brain cancer but had become blind as a consequence of the treatment. Unable to come to terms with his disability, Tyler was isolated and fearful, drowning in a depression so deep he would not interact with other children.

Paulette, Lana, and Grizzly sat quietly as the children in Tyler's class filed in one by one from recess. A little girl who could see shadows demanded to know what the bulky body on the floor was. Learning that it was a dog, the children felt their way to Grizzly and crowded around him to run their hands lightly over his body—all except Tyler. The minute Tyler entered the room, he groped his way along the wall until he reached a far corner where, barricaded behind a long table and child-sized chairs, he huddled down, knees drawn up, his face hidden in his arms. Grizzly patiently accepted the blind children's exploration, but he kept turning his head in Tyler's direction and air-scenting.

The moment came when he could stand it no longer. With exquisite slowness so as not to topple the children, Grizzly rose to his feet, and when all the small hands had fallen away, he stepped free of the circle of children and approached the table that served Tyler as a fortress. He dropped to his belly and worked with his muzzle to push aside a chair, crawled a short way under the table until his progress was blocked by another chair and nosed that aside. Left and right, he pushed the chairs aside until he reached Tyler. Making himself as small as he could and speaking in his throat with soft little woofing sounds, he cuddled up next to the boy and placed his head slowly and gently in the boy's lap. Fearfully, Tyler's hands explored Grizzly's head. "It's a dog," he whispered. Grizzly woofled that he had guessed correctly and inched closer. Little by little, Tyler relaxed. "It's a dog and he's my friend," he murmured.

After a time Lana asked, "Tyler, would you like to bring your friend out and introduce him to the other children? You can call him Grizzly and give them permission to touch him. I imagine they'd like that, and he won't mind as long as you're there with him."

It did not happen immediately, but happen it did. Tyler took hold of Grizzly's harness, and Grizzly, walking slowly and carefully, led the way back to the center of the room. Tyler stood there with his arm proprietarily around Grizzly's neck and talked with the other children about his new friend.

After that, there was no question that volunteers from The Good Shepherd Association would be welcome at the school. Not only had Grizzly succeeded where human intervention had failed, but the staff could envision another benefit from having dogs visit. When the children got older, they would be eligible to have guide dogs, and the more familiarity they gained with dogs before then, the more likely was the pairing to be a success.

"There's no way of training Onyx or any other dog to do what Grizzly did this morning," Paulette said in the car on the way home.

"But Onyx will have special things that only she does. So will Megan. All animals are teachers and healers in their own way. I firmly believe that," Lana said, and Paulette agreed that it might be so.

A curriculum for volunteers was mapped out, with Lana concentrating on the people side and Paulette the animal side. The curriculum was designed to be taught in two-hour seminars held one evening a week for eight weeks. Included was instruction in how to work with professionals (such as nurses, therapists, teachers, and physical therapists), what information about the patient or client the handlers were entitled to ask for and the information they could usefully contribute in return, and the medical and psychological terminology they should be familiar with. How to approach clients, both children and adults, was stressed, along with the need to be professional at all times. To that end the training emphasized that volunteers had to be utterly responsible about keeping appointments and showing up on time prepared to work, and responsible too about keeping any promises made to clients, such as offering to bring a snapshot of the dog that a child could keep. One of the most important training points, referred to again and again, was the necessity for strict confidentiality. The volunteers could *not* go home and talk about clients they had seen that day, describe cases, refer to case histories, tell anecdotes about their work, or dine out on interesting stories. Just as much as any other member of the health team, they had to respect the patients' privacy.

One way of having the volunteers seen not as casual visitors but as auxiliary members of the health team, Lana and Paulette decided, was to have them wear some sort of uniform, which would be neat and clean and would identify them, along with the Delta Society ID card they carried. Similarly, dogs were not to be decked out in funny hats or eyeglasses—no costumes of any sort—but were to bear identification as therapy dogs. A logo was designed consisting of the outline of a heart with a profile of Grizzly superimposed and the words THE GOOD SHEPHERD ASSOCIATION circling his head. Deep red T-shirts with this logo on the front and the words PAWS HELPING PEOPLE on the back were ordered. These were to be worn by the handlers, and neck scarves with the logo were to be worn by the dogs, white for a dog in training, red for a graduate.

The strictest possible standards for cleanliness were established. Handlers had to know how to groom their animals, to clip and file their nails, clean their ears, and brush their teeth. Within twenty-four hours of taking the dogs to a therapy session, they had to bathe them and rub them down with an antidander preparation. Because disease transmission between animals and humans is possible, although it occurs more often from humans to animals than the other way around, the dogs had to be up-to-date on their vaccinations and any other preventive measures needed to keep them healthy. When being transported, the dogs had to be crated or have a seat belt fastened around them. As important as the dog's safety and health was the animal's emotional health, so handlers had to learn to recognize signs of stress and agree never to work their dogs for more than an hour at a time.

As the training of volunteers got under way, Lana and Paulette found that dog owners coming from an obedience training background presented the biggest challenge because their focus was to mold the behavior of the animal, to shape the dog to respond quickly and consistently to commands, while therapy work required dogs who were sensitive to situations and able to modify their behavior accordingly. It apparently did not occur to the owner of a dog trained to obedience to wonder if the commands given made sense to the animal—if the dog saw any reason for what it was being ordered to do. The task with such owners—and they were the majority of the volunteers because they had made the rounds of shows and obedience trials and now were looking for some new activity to engage in—was to refocus their notion that dogs were to be ordered about. Instead, they had to accept the idea that their dogs could be teachers as well as learners: that while human beings might teach them, the dogs had much to teach human beings as well.

"What we have to do," Lana would tell the volunteers, "is sit back and listen and watch our animals rather than impose our rigid rules of behavior and obedience. Get rid of the ego approach that dictates that you have to have a *good* dog, the *best* dog, the dog that *wins ribbons,* and begin to think of your dog as your partner. He or she is your working teammate, and what you ask must make sense *to the dog.* Animals have minds and use them. We need to observe them, watch their behavior, learn all we can about them; they already are experts in knowing us."

Lana would describe how she herself took Grizzly for granted, underestimating him as "just a dog," until the afternoon he went into the closet for her running shoes and brought them to her. "That taught me," she said, "that animals can think, that having four legs doesn't make animals less than we are, only different."

The advice given in the seminars was this: Lie down on the floor with your animal. Just lie beside him quietly; don't expect the animal to do anything with you. Touch him. Touch him lightly and gently all over. Try to talk to him nonverbally. Repeat the words silently in your head and leave yourself open for his answer. Have quiet contact with the animal in a meditative way. During the day, go everywhere with your animal that you can. Be with him while he eats, and have him sit beside you while you eat. Learn his environment. Try to see what it looks like through his eyes.

At the same time, remember that an animal, like a person, needs privacy and space. The dog needs a bed of his own and a space that belongs to him. Play with your animal. Learn what makes your animal happy. Learn to identify your animal's emotions, for he can certainly identify yours. Be open to the animal's teaching you. The energy should go both ways, with an equal exchange of information between the two of you.

As Lana and Paulette gained experience, they discovered that it was not the breed that determined a good therapy dog but the dog's own personality. Some dogs seemed destined to work with people, and it had nothing to do with whether the dog was a thoroughbred or had come from a shelter. In fact, dogs adopted from a shelter sometimes seemed particularly qualified, perhaps because they had known adversity and, like people who have been through tragedy, were sensitive to the troubles of others.

Dogs who end up in shelters have lost the people and places they belonged to. They probably feel abandoned and terrified of what is to become of them. Then the right human being walks by and there is an immediate connection between person and animal—eye contact, nonverbal communication. Trust and acceptance spring up on both sides. The animal senses that he or she will be loved and understood because the person has responded to the animal's goodness. The owner who adopts a dog from a shelter recognizes the animal's strength and originality, while the owner who buys a dog from a kennel usually is concerned with the animal's breed and conformation and may be indifferent to inner qualities.

Lana and Paulette learned that the relationship of the volunteer and the animal was crucial to whether they made a successful therapy team. The relationship had to be deep and trusting and, in a special sense, equal. The dog had to trust the owner to keep him or her safe, and the owner had to have confidence that the dog would behave appropriately. Much of the training that Paulette developed was designed to foster this sort of trust between handler and dog. Small groups of handlers and dogs, with Paulette and Onyx or Lana and Grizzly leading them, went to downtown Salt Lake City, to the airport, and to malls to accustom the dogs to crowds and all sorts of sights and smells and sounds. The dogs were taken on buses, into the public spaces of hospitals and nursing homes, into elevators, onto moving sidewalks, and to places with different kinds of floor coverings: rugs, tiles, gratings. If special permission for training purposes was granted by the owner of the establishment, the dogs accompanied the handlers into restaurants. They also accompanied their handlers into rest rooms, not just as far as the washbasins but into the stalls. Lana remembers with amusement the day she entered a rest room to be greeted by the sight of the front paws of five dogs sticking out from under five doors. It was to desensitize the dogs to the smell of human urine and fecal matter which they would encounter in working with brain-injured patients that it was recommended that dogs always accompany the handler into the bathroom.

If a dog reacted to some particular sight or smell, the handler was instructed to desensitize the animal slowly and in small increments by repeated exposure to the stimulus while at the same time providing large amounts of reassurance and support. Most alarming to some dogs is the smell of blood because it indicates an injury. Lana described how she cut her finger in the kitchen and Grizzly came quickly from another room, wanting to fix the cut by licking it. Not until Lana showed him the finger, washed clean and covered by a Band-Aid, did he return to his interrupted nap.

Even when not formally engaged in training, volunteers were encouraged to keep their dogs with them as much as possible. Lana spoke of her own experience of taking Grizzly to classes. It had prompted her to see the campus—bicycles, skateboards, runners, Frisbees flying through the air—through a dog's eyes, and she felt that Grizzly, in turn, learned to view these things with something approximating the vision of a person. "We exchanged education as we walked on campus," she told the volunteers. "Training is not something that is accomplished and is then over. It is ongoing, never-ending education."

Dogs are not concerned with looks, the volunteers were reminded. A person can be deformed, mutilated, homely, or dirty, that's all right with a dog. Usually it makes no difference if the person is young or old, although some dogs have a liking for children and some—Grizzly, for one—prefer not to have to cope with anyone under one year of age. Grizzly tolerated infants like he tolerated puppies, sniffing them but not having anything more to do with them than that. When he and Lana began to work in a setting dealing with developmentally disabled children, Lana could, and often did, place a young child against him as he lay on his side; but he never woofled to such a child, and if the child cried, he wanted, like most males, to have a woman come and take over.

Before accepting a dog and owner into the handler training classes, Lana and Paulette evaluated the animal for skills and basic attitude, and in the course of the training they continued to observe both animal and handler for how they interacted and how they handled stress. The seminars were held in a long-term rehabilitation facility owned and operated by a health maintenance organization, and Paulette with Onyx, Cheryl with Megan, and Lana with Grizzly all volunteered there. The physical therapists working with accident and stroke victims were so persuaded of the value of animal-assisted therapy that management was happy to loan The Good Shepherd Association a meeting room for the seminars. The room was large, enabling Paulette to demonstrate training techniques and the handlers to practice them then and there; the facility itself was educational, for it gave the dogs a chance to get used to waxed floors, doors that opened automatically, and hospital sights, sounds, and smells. In the corridors, the handlers could practice having the dogs walk on their right side rather than the left as the dogs had originally been taught in obedience training. Wheelchairs were available for the dogs to learn to pull, as well as beds that the dogs learned to approach quietly, while avoiding medical equipment, and to climb up on, not by jumping but by putting their front legs on the bed and waiting for their hindquarters to be lifted. They learned to lie still for long periods of time, to ignore other therapy dogs, which they would need to know when more than one team at a time went to a facility, and to allow themselves to be handled all over without protest. The handler was always to be at the animal's side to ward off hurt, but a child might strike a dog without warning, as happened to Grizzly one day when an autistic boy smashed his fist down between Grizzly's eyes. A therapy dog had to be able to accept such an attack without retaliating.

Role-playing was used in the seminars to illustrate ways of approaching patients. With someone acting the part of an overactive child, an unresponsive adult, or a stroke-damaged patient, Lana would model words that could be used and ways of handling a particular situation. She emphasized that the handler should be alert to any cues the dog was giving and used an incident involving Grizzly as a case in point. A sweet old woman had had a stroke and was unable to sit up. Her physical therapist, who wanted to encourage her to use her left arm, led the way into the room saying, "Mrs. Boone, would you like to see Grizzly today?" Mrs. Boone replied, "That would be nice," and the therapist gave Lana the go-ahead sign. The two of them placed a drawsheet on the bed and settled Grizzly on the bed beside Mrs. Boone where she could see and pet him.

"What I didn't know," Lana told the handlers, "was that this was a very compliant woman who always agreed pleasantly to anything anyone suggested. When Grizzly got on the bed, the woman kept smiling but she was awkward about petting him and Grizzly kept turning his head away. He didn't want to look at her and he wouldn't speak. He just kept averting his face, and it was clear he wanted to get off the bed. Later, the therapist told me that after we left, the patient said, 'I was awfully afraid that big dog was going to bite me.' Grizzly knew the woman was frightened of him—that's why he kept turning his head away—and if I'd paid attention to what Griz was trying to tell me, I'd have known it too."

Had there once been something else, something far more important, that Griz tried to tell her but that she had failed to recognize? Lana wondered about that after a day early in their acquaintance when Paulette remarked that she had the impression there was something wrong with Grizzly's eyes and suggested taking him to a veterinarian she knew of who was an expert in the treatment of eye problems. Lana did so—and was thoroughly unprepared for the news the specialist gave her.

"Grizzly is blind," he said.

"No. No, he can't be," she stammered. "I would have known."

"Not necessarily. If he were a person, the term would be 'legally blind.' That is to say, he can make out shadows and shapes. Dogs are far less dependent on eyesight than humans are. They rely on their sense of smell, and their hearing is acute, so they can compensate a great deal for not being able to see. Also, his blindness may have been coming on gradually for some time. Was he ever in an accident?"

Lana's mind flashed back to the moment of Jeremy's death. Grizzly had raced down the stairs and out the front door, into the side of a passing car.

"Yes, that's probably when it started," the doctor said. "But even if the injury had been apparent, you had more, much more, to deal with than a dog who'd gotten a bump in the head."

Lana thought of the two years when she had scarcely been aware of anything. No, it was not surprising that she had not been aware that Grizzly's sight was going. Or gone. But since then, with the remarkable things he had done? Well, as incredible as it seemed, yes, he must have been relying on his nose and ears, and shadows and shapes, and sharpened awareness of everything around him to give him the information he then acted on.

When she got home, she called Dave, at work, and then Ella. "Ella," she said, "I have something very sad to tell you. Grizzly is blind."

There was a silence. Then Ella, with her comforting, positive attitude, said, "I always knew Grizzly was special, but I didn't know just how special."

"Nor did I."

They talked for a while, Ella remembering incidents Lana had told her about, Lana adding more incidents, incidents that seemed even more amazing now they knew Grizzly could not see. "Of course," Ella said finally, "it may be that we're looking at this the wrong way around. We're saying isn't it remarkable what Grizzly can do despite not being able to see. But maybe he responds so sensitively *because* he can't see. Maybe he relies on something deeper than sight to let him know the right thing to do."

"Insight rather than sight?"

"Yes."

"Yes," Lana said. "I think that must be it."

And in her heart she added, *Thank you, Ella, for your own insight. I couldn't have come this far without it.*

8
The Christmas Visit

Lana and Paulette quickly learned to question volunteers about their reasons for being interested in doing animal-assisted therapy. "What brought you here?" they asked. "Why do you want to do this work?" If they detected in the answers that the volunteer was, perhaps unconsciously, looking for means to work out a personal problem, they found tactful ways of turning the volunteer down. If the person came across as self-centered, as someone seeking opportunities to say, in effect, Hey, look at me; look at my dog, that person too was discouraged from embarking on the training.

Because dogs and children are the stuff of good human interest stories, the media quickly caught on to the existence of The Good Shepherd Association (TGSA), and items in newspapers and on local TV caught the attention of people desirous of the spotlight. Such people were plainly told that the work was not a dog show, that it did not involve competing with other handlers, that, indeed, it was quite solitary for the most part: The handler went to the assignment alone, checked in alone, and left alone, and when handlers went home they could not recount events in their day or anecdotes about the people they served because confidentiality was the organization's strongest rule. To reinforce the point, Lana sometimes described how she and Dave had been at the movies one evening and before the film started overheard two women seated behind them talking about an abused child. One of the women was apparently a student aide working at a psychiatric facility where Lana and Grizzly volunteered, and she was passing on intimate details about the family of a child Lana could readily identify from the description.

"The client has a right to privacy, which means that talk about a client can only be done with another professional, and then only on a need-to-know basis," Lana cautioned prospective volunteers. "Violating this rule means immediate dismissal from the Association. By the same token, if you are out in public—shopping at the mall, say—and you encounter a client, you do not acknowledge that you have met unless the client speaks to you. Even then you must only say hello and how are you and not mention anything bearing on your relationship in the therapeutic setting."

Dog owners who heard about animal-assisted therapy were sometimes drawn to the idea because it meant they would get to take their dogs to places like hospitals where animals were ordinarily forbidden to go, plus the dogs would be given more respect than the average pet. If a woman had competed in a number of dog shows and winning titles no longer excited her, she might be looking around for something new to do with the dog and was aware that the dog was capable of more than bringing home ribbons and had something special to give. Handlers tended to understand their dogs in depth because they had worked long and closely with them. Better than the average owner with a pet in the house, they knew the intelligence and heart of the animal. The person who said, when asked to give a reason for volunteering, "Because I think my dog is unusually responsive, because she's good with people, because there is a comforting quality about her," was a person Lana and Paulette welcomed.

Occasionally, a prospective volunteer had a reason that had at least as much to do with the dog owner as the dog. Such was the case with one early volunteer. This woman, who worked for a large corporation as a computer programmer, had nearly died of breast cancer. She knew all too well what it was like to have a life completely changed by illness, and she wanted to give back some of what she had been given in the way of love and support when she was ill. One of the first things she had done when she was well enough was to rescue a dog nobody wanted from a shelter. Maggie was a golden retriever, a beautiful dog but so timid that she would urinate whenever she became nervous. Her new and gentle owner thought she had cured Maggie of that, but when Maggie was being tested for her potential as a therapy dog, the submissive peeing came on again.

Paulette responded sensitively, telling the volunteer, "You've done a lot of good work with her. Let's see if we can get her past this problem with just a little bit more." Paulette worked out the ways, Maggie and her owner came through the eight weeks of training with flying colors, and the two of them went to work with brain-injured patients. This work requires tremendous patience, a quality the team had in good measure.

Another woman had a story to tell when asked her reason for volunteering. Several years before, when her son was fourteen, the two of them were vacationing at a campground and a scruffy little nondescript mutt came around begging for food. The boy took a liking to Scruffy and begged his mother to be allowed to keep him, badgering her so that she told him if he so much as mentioned the dog one more time, the answer was no, but that if he would shut up about it, she would give the matter some thought. On the day they packed to go home, the boy watched his mother with ever-growing anxiety but said nothing. Even when she told him to get in the car while she took a last look around, he did not burst into pleading, only seemed to be near tears. His mother got in the car, started the engine, and then, reaching in her carryall, she said, "Oh, by the way, is this what you wanted?" and handed Scruffy across to the boy. Now the tears did come, but they were tears of joy.

Scruffy proved to be a grand and grateful dog, utterly devoted to his master, and when the boy, at seventeen and taking a short-cut through a construction site, was killed by a car, both Scruffy and the boy's mother were devastated. It was another year before the woman began to look outward again. When she did and heard about The Good Shepherd Association, she thought that here was a way to use Scruffy's pent-up love and her own to benefit other children.

Dogs were not the only animals to be presented for testing for their suitability to become therapy animals. Two cats and a lop-eared bunny named Buttercup qualified and proved valuable when the client, by reason of age or vulnerability, really could only benefit from the warmth and tactile stimulation of a furry body pressed close. The most exotic of the therapy animals was a llama belonging to the widow of a university professor who lived in a farmlike setting with llamas and standard poodles. Charlie, the llama, was housebroken, enjoyed being bathed in warm water, and was perfectly agreeable to being walked with a halter. His huge eyes and soft lips, which always appeared to be smiling, delighted the patients when Charlie appeared at rehabilitation facilities. He could only go when other therapy teams were not present, however, because the dogs did not know what to make of Charlie and were too distracted to work well when he was around.

It did not take Lana and Paulette long to realize that testing the animals was only part of the process of getting new handlers ready to go into the field. The animals seemed to sense instinctively what to do. The more difficult task was to make sure the handlers had the necessary skills. The one-day seminar that Lana taught for the Delta Society was sufficient to prepare people to do simple visits to facilities such as nursing homes, but in order to work with more emotionally and physically fragile populations, the volunteers needed much more training. Over the next couple of years, Lana and Paulette gradually developed a training program that evolved into a tightly organized class conducted one evening a week for eight weeks.

When the volunteers completed this obligatory eight-week course of training, both dogs and handlers were tested. The dogs had to demonstrate their ability to shake hands, speak on command, approach a bed, pull a wheelchair, and tolerate all sorts of handling with total patience. Handlers for their part were given a written exam to test their understanding of commonly used medical and psychiatric terms and their ability to respond appropriately in various hypothetical situations. There were questions dealing with seizure disorders, infection control issues, and the handling of abused children, along with others concerned with small but vital points, such as why not to wear jewelry when dealing with autistic children (they are distracted by the glitter). The handlers also had to demonstrate their ability to keep their animals in top-notch condition.

With successful completion of the training, volunteer and dog were assigned to work with an experienced handler, and the two teams visited a facility together until the mentor was satisfied that the volunteer was knowledgeable about the techniques required by the facility and both handler and dog were comfortable about executing them. This could require as brief a time as three weeks or as long a time as six months. The type of facility to which they were assigned was based on the volunteer's choice and the dog's capabilities. Dogs who were obedience-trained, for instance, enjoyed working in a rehabilitation setting because they were accustomed to responding to commands and happily pulled wheelchairs, retrieved tossed balls, and went for walks, while quieter, more sensitively attuned dogs were often well-suited for work in a psychiatric setting. As for the handlers, someone who was willing to work in a very hands-on way might be assigned to a school for deaf and blind children, while the opposite sort of person, someone who was able to listen and observe carefully and empathetically, was better suited to work with abused children. But first consideration was always given to the handler's own preference.

Lana and Paulette observed the handlers and the dogs throughout the training sessions and developed educated guesses about the work they were best suited for, but not until the team was in the field could they be certain whether their hunches were correct. It was up to the mentor to report back whether the handler could deal with the unexpected, could analyze a situation and make good decisions, and was assertive enough to recommend an alternative to the therapist if what was being asked was not safe for the animal to do. For example, if the therapist proposed to place a child on the dog's back, the handler had to be able to speak up and veto the idea because it would put too much pressure on the animal's spine—a dog is not a horse to be ridden—plus there was the additional danger that the child might fall off. It was up to the handler to ask, "What is the goal for this child?", and if the therapist said it was sensory stimulation through full body contact with the dog, the handler could say, "Fine. We can do it this way," and cradle the child against the animal in a way that was safe for both.

The handler was also expected to be assertive enough to request a briefing session by the therapist before meeting with a regular patient in order to be updated on the patient's progress after the last session and be told the goal for the current session. Knowing the goal, the handler could then determine the activity or technique to be used. For example, the physical therapist might report that the right arm of a stroke patient had become stronger and in this session they needed to work on the left arm and on the patient's fine-motor skills. With this information, the handler might decide to have the patient toss a ball left-handed for the dog to retrieve and then pick up a biscuit from a tray and hold it out to the dog as a reward for bringing the ball back. After the session the handler needed to request debriefing: Was the goal met? What were the recommendations for the next session? If the session had been with children and the therapist proposed to work on colors the next time, the handler would make a note, for example, to bring red and green dog biscuits in small and large sizes the next time so the children had the task of choosing the color called for to reward the dog.

All handlers were asked to supply written documentation of each session, with one copy going to the facility and a second for the Association files. The documentation included when they checked in and out of a session; how many clients they saw; what equipment, if any, was used; what techniques were employed; were the techniques successful; and, if not, what was done to solve the problem. The handlers were also asked to note the stress level of the animal they were working with; for example, "Fluffy seemed relaxed and happy" or "Fluffy seemed restless today." As might be expected, getting volunteers to turn in reports was an ongoing challenge.

Lana looked through every report that came in to determine if any safety issues were involved, whether the techniques used were relevant to the stated goals, and whether a handler had devised a new approach that perhaps should be taught to others. One such technique came about in work with a brain-injured patient. The physical therapist, saying she wanted the patient to stretch his gnarled arms, suggested that the dog play tug-of-war with him, which the handler vetoed as too aggressive an approach. Instead she suggested that there be a therapist on each side of the patient to make certain that he was not pulled over and that she position herself alongside the dog with both hands on his collar. When all was in readiness, the handler slowly moved the dog away, providing a finely controlled stretch to the patient's arms in a way that the patient, who was usually full of groans and protests, actually enjoyed because a dog, not a machine, was involved. The technique was such a success that it was videotaped by the facility to familiarize other therapists and handlers with its use.

Another bit of problem-solving evolved when it was observed that tears came to the eyes of a little boy whenever he threw a ball for the therapy dog to retrieve. Ordinarily a small child delights in having a large dog obey his command to fetch. Why was this child different? In the debriefing that followed the session, the therapist mentioned that he was a child who had been ritualistically and sexually abused. The authorities had taken him away from his mother and later, for an assortment of reasons, he had to be removed from each of the foster homes he was placed in, which meant that every time he grew attached to someone or something, it was taken away from him.

Lana attended the next session and asked the child to throw a ball for Grizzly. She saw the tears start and the little boy appear to shrink down into himself. Grizzly, too, behaved oddly in that he could not seem to find the ball. Although his sense of smell enabled him to find anything he wanted to, this time he just stood around and woofled plaintively.

"What's he saying?" the boy asked Lana.

"Maybe he wants you to come and help him find the ball," she guessed. A sudden flash of intuition told her the guess was exactly right. The ball represented to the boy all the times he himself had been thrown away, and Grizzly's going after it represented his being abandoned. Grizzly sensed that, Lana thought, as she watched the boy and dog hunt for the ball together; he seemed to know that retrieving the ball himself was the wrong thing to do. The boy needed to be with him, hunting for it, not just passively waiting for him to return. It was yet another time when she acknowledged to herself, This dog knows more than I do.

Lana, of course, said nothing to the child, simply modified the activity to things boy and dog could do together. She explained her reasoning and offered her insights to the boy's psychotherapist after the session because, as she repeatedly stressed to the volunteers, they were there to assist, not replace, the therapist.

Throughout the first year of The Good Shepherd Association, Lana and Paulette experimented, observed, improvised, identified problems, sought solutions, and formulated standards for animal-assisted treatment. Each had special strengths that allowed them to complement the other. Lana had experienced at first hand the intense emotional and physical pain many of their clients lived with, and she understood far better than most people the problems these clients faced. Paulette, on the other hand, had a lifetime of experience in training and handling a wide variety of animals, ranging from dolphins to dogs. This is not to say that their talents and dedication always resulted in a smooth relationship, however. Disagreements occurred, and questions of organizational policies and structure tended to occupy much more time and effort than they had anticipated.

Neither Lana nor Paulette had any management experience, and establishing an effective governing board to guide the organization proved to be a formidable task. The Good Shepherd Association predictably attracted individuals with a strong interest in animals but had a harder time drawing in individuals with expertise in management, fund-raising, and the like. As a result, clear staff guidelines, program goals, and budgetary priorities were never laid down. At the heart of most of the governance and management issues that came up was the question of whether The Good Shepherd Association was to be a kind of club or a professional human service organization. From the beginning, Lana had envisioned a professional caregiving agency, while Paulette had assumed that because the handlers were volunteers, the standards would be more relaxed. This philosophical difference eventually had disastrous repercussions, but at this point it was no more than a small cloud on an otherwise bright horizon.

By the end of the first year of its existence, The Good Shepherd Association had gone from three to twenty teams of handler and animal, with the animal members including three German shepherds, a Doberman, three Rottweilers, a sheltie, two golden retrievers, two Labrador retrievers, an Australian shepherd, several mixed breeds, two cats, and the lop-eared rabbit. A board of directors of the Association had been constituted, with Dave Davis initially serving as acting board chairman because he had years of experience in working with nonprofit human services organizations. The Association registered with the State of Utah as an incorporated charitable association and was granted tax-exempt status by the Internal Revenue Service. Because the handlers had all been certified by the Delta Society, each team was covered by Delta's liability insurance.

With the organization growing so rapidly and demanding so much of her time, thought, and energy, Lana decided to postpone her goal of earning a college degree and pursue this more urgent dream of making animal-assisted therapy an accepted and effective treatment modality in a wide range of health care and mental health care settings. As the executive director of TGSA, she took on all the day-to-day responsibilities of manning an office, coordinating a growing volunteer staff, training and supporting volunteer handlers, and developing and monitoring programs in the various facilities the organization served. Paulette worked half-time, primarily at training new volunteers, and a part-time bookkeeper kept the books. Dave advised Lana on management issues and did the majority of the fund-raising for the Association.

A newsletter, *Paws Helping People*, was started to provide news about the organization to supporters in the community, keep members in touch with what was going on and bring everyone up to date on policies being formulated, such as, that dogs should not be permitted to socialize before a session when teams were working together. Paulette wrote a monthly column of training tips, and a veterinarian provided a column on health and safety guidelines. There were also monthly membership meetings, to which members could bring their animals for socialization and further training, where issues of training and comportment were discussed and new techniques were demonstrated. A typical topic might be: How to know when to call in sick on behalf of your pet partner. Like people, a dog might not feel like going to work on a particular day, and the owner needed to be able to recognize subtle signs of depression or lethargy or listlessness. Owners also needed to be alert to the first signs of illness by checking during a normal grooming session for lumps, sores, hair loss, weight gain or loss, and odors or discharges. If the animal needed a veterinarian's care, it was a rule of TSGA that a written release from the veterinarian stating the diagnosis, treatment, and prognosis of the illness had to be obtained before the animal resumed work.

Some handlers had more than one dog and could substitute one pet partner for another if a particular animal seemed out of sorts or if one animal was better suited than another to a specific type of work. One man had four dogs, ranging in temperament from highly active to passive and serene, which allowed him to match the needs of the client with the appropriate dog. As owners are well aware, animals, like people, have differing personalities and thus differing things to offer.

Recognizing the value of having more than one therapy animal, Lana asked Ella Brown to reserve a puppy for her, a female this time, to be a companion for Grizzly. This Ella did, and some months later the puppy arrived from Oregon. Lana named her Kodyella, in part in honor of Ella herself, whose generous gift to Jeremy was now reverberating through so many lives.

A high point of the second year of The Good Shepherd Association was a Christmas visit to a children's hospital that was requested by the hospital as a special treat for the patients. Paulette and Lana gathered together ten of their best handlers for an orientation session in which they described what the handlers were likely to see and how they might best interact with the children. Avoid focusing on the children's appearance, the handlers were told. Maintain a positive attitude and stay in the present. Kids don't need to recollect how things used to be or how they might be in the future. Concentrate on the here and now, and on making this a happy experience.

At two on a December afternoon, the handlers and their animals, including Buttercup, the rabbit, met in the lobby of the hospital. After Paulette had checked them all, they walked upstairs to the third floor, where the children were waiting for the animals to arrive. Some of the patients were in strollers, some in wheelchairs, and one who had been in a car accident and was in traction was wheeled in in his bed. Some children were hooked to an IV pole. Some had no hair. Some were swathed in bandages. Some were carrying emesis basins. But they all grinned when the dogs came strolling in.

The children petted the dogs, hugged and kissed them, and fed them treats. Children in wheelchairs were given a pull around the room. Candy canes were passed out, and Dave took Polaroid pictures of each child with the dog (or rabbit) of his or her choice. The photos, along with a Good Shepherd necklace and a teddy bear, went to each child as a remembrance of this happy time. The handlers, the children, the hospital personnel, perhaps even the dogs and Buttercup, counted the visit a grand success.

About seven that evening, Lana got a call from the hospital's child-life therapist. "I made a terrible mistake today," he said, "and I'm wondering if I can ask you to help me. A little boy who hasn't much time left was really looking forward to seeing the dogs, but he was asleep when they came and we overlooked bringing him to the recreation room. His mother says Simon has been brave all week, not crying or complaining on the promise of seeing the dogs, but when he found he had missed them, he began to sob. The nurses don't know if he will make it through the night. Do you think someone could possibly come now?"

Lana quickly ran down in her mind which handler might be available, who would have a dog ready, who could deal with a dying boy. "How much time do I have to get someone?"

"Not much. None, really. The boy has been unhooked from the life support systems."

So little time meant Grizzly and she would have to go, Lana realized. But not alone. She would need to have someone with her. She called Bruce Wignal, who had two children of his own. He and Aspen, his golden retriever, were the best team working with children. "Bruce, I've got a special assignment," she said. "This is the situation. Can you make it?"

"Aspen's ready to go," he said. "We can leave in five minutes. What is it you want me to do?"

His own two-year-old had recently been in the hospital. Lana said, "Just do what you would do if it were your son."

"Okay, I'll be there."

It had been snowing during the day and now it was icy, but Lana and Grizzly and Bruce and Aspen made it through to the hospital. The child-life therapist met them in the lobby and hustled them to the stairwell and up the stairs because it was against hospital rules for dogs to make a bedside visit, although in this case special permission had been obtained from the head nurse. The therapist led them to the little boy's room and quietly opened the door.

"The dogs are here. Is he . . . ?" The boy's mother nodded and tried to smile. The boy himself had a sheet drawn up to his chin, and his large brown eyes were staring straight ahead.

Lana went to the side of the bed. "Hello, Simon. I have a couple of special friends here who would like to visit with you. This is Grizzly; he's a big German shepherd. Aspen is a golden retriever. Would you like to see them?"

Almost imperceptibly, the boy's head nodded. Lana had Grizzly put his front paws up on the bed and Bruce, at the foot of the bed, had Aspen follow suit. Simon's eyes got even bigger as he stared at the dogs. His mother beamed through the weariness that showed in the deep dark circles under her eyes. "Oh, thank you for coming," she whispered. "Simon has tried all week to be a good boy and not to cry. He knew the dogs were coming and he would get to see them if he didn't cry. Then we found out he'd slept through the visit and it broke his heart. I'm so sorry to bring you out like this."

"We're delighted to be here," Lana said.

And Bruce added, "Thank you for thinking of us."

"Simon," Lana said, "would you like Grizzly to lie beside you so you can pet him?" Again the tiny nod came. "Okay, we need to scoot you over a little bit." Simon's mother helped to move the paper-thin boy and place a drawsheet on the bed. Grizzly put his forepaws on the bed, and as Lana lifted his hindquarters up he inched his way into position. His body, longer than the boy's, touched along the boy's length, and he tucked his nose into the hollow beneath the boy's shoulder. Simon moved his hand to pet Griz with a touch as light as a blade of grass moving in a breeze.

A nurse burst into the room. "His vitals are skyrocketing!"

"Oh, my gosh, I'm sorry," Lana said. "Do you want the dog off?"

"No, no, you're okay."

"If Simon just keeps petting him, I'm sure they'll go down," Lana said, basing her assurance on the fact that a great deal of research shows that petting an animal reduces heart rate and blood pressure. Both the nurse and the boy's mother were smiling broadly, which struck Lana as weird, but she did not know what move to make so she suggested to Grizzly that he talk to Simon, which he did very softly in his throat. Bruce followed the nurse out of the room to get his gear bag, and when he came back in he too was smiling. He put Aspen up on the bed on the other side of the boy and took Polaroid pictures of the three, which he gave to Simon, while Lana told Simon that whenever he wanted he could close his eyes and think of how soft Griz and Aspen were and how much they liked him. To remind him, Grizzly and Aspen would leave one of their friends with him, a fuzzy teddy bear, and the bear would sleep with him to keep him company.

The nurses' station with its bank of monitors was right outside the door. "What did we do wrong?" Lana asked when she and Bruce came out of Simon's room with the dogs.

The nurse explained that when Grizzly had gotten up on the bed, the boy's heart rate, his blood pressure, and his respiration rate all shot up to normal. "That's what I meant when I said sky-rocketing. They went up to normal!"

The child-life therapist thanked Lana and Bruce over and over as he escorted them down to the lobby. Out in the cold night air, Lana and Bruce said little, their hearts heavy for the boy who would be gone by morning and yet glad because they had been able to give a few moments of happiness and comfort to a dying child and his grieving mother.

9
Loving Connection

As the reputation of The Good Shepherd Association spread, various types of facilities became interested in participating in the program. One was a halfway house for women who were substance abusers—of either drugs or alcohol. Their children were in residence too, and the animal-assisted therapy was wanted for them. As the head therapist told Lana, the children were as much in need of treatment as their mothers.

"They've been in dysfunctional families," she said. "Their parents are users—if they have two parents, that is; most of them don't. The children have been neglected. What upbringing they've had has been erratic. We'd like you to come and work with us to see if we can get these kids to open up, to trust, to learn self-care skills and become socialized."

It was a tall order, and Lana hesitated. "Let me bring Grizzly in and assess the situation."

Curiously enough, one of the mothers proved more disruptive than any of the children. Not much more than a child herself, Marietta begged to be allowed in the therapy room with the children and the dog. "Oh, please," she pleaded. "*Please* let me see Grizzly. *Please!*" There seemed little to do but agree. The minute

Marietta was inside the room, she lay down on the floor beside Grizzly and wrapped her arms around him. "I feel so calm with him," she said dreamily. "I feel so happy."

The therapist finally persuaded her off the floor and onto a couch, where she watched enviously as the children examined every inch of Grizzly, from his teeth to his feet. Then Marietta's daughter happened to do something her mother did not like and Marietta reached out and snatched her by the arm, yanking her into midair and yelling, "Get over here!"

Grizzly sat up abruptly and turned his head toward the mother. He could not see Marietta but she did not know that, and his seeming stare froze her in place.

"Oh, I'm sorry," she faltered.

Grizzly cocked his head. "*Wuh-wuh-wuh-wuh*," he scolded.

Lana interceded. "You know what works with Grizzly when he's doing something I don't want him to do? I say, 'Griz, would you please come over here? I'd like for you to come and do this instead.'"

Griz turned to Lana approvingly. "*Muh-muh-muh*."

"He's so funny," Marietta giggled. "You're right, though. That's what I should do, isn't it?" This mentoring of mothering skills led to the young woman's being included in the animal-assisted therapy sessions when Lana agreed that TGSA would serve at the facility.

With the children, Lana used techniques that had been worked out with other children in group treatment. For a lesson in similarities, she had the children sit on little rugs in a circle around Grizzly and compare his toes to their toes. How many toes does he have? How many do you have? What is the difference between his toes and yours? To teach them to share, she brought just two brushes so the children had to take turns brushing the dog. Because Grizzly would not respond if they shouted or spoke harshly, the children learned that when they wanted something, they had to ask nicely for it, to say, "Grizzly, please sit," and afterward, "Thank you for sitting, Grizzly." If a child's self-esteem was low, Grizzly made the child work a little. If the child said, "Please sit" and Grizzly immediately sat, that was all there was to it, but if the child had to work at it, there was a real sense of accomplishment when finally Grizzly obeyed. The same was true if a child did not speak clearly. The child had to stand in front of Grizzly and articulate the commands—Go down . . . stand up . . . take the treat . . . shake my hand—in a firm voice before Grizzly would comply.

To have the children learn about animals and that animals have feelings, Lana had the children stand absolutely still and put their arms out to pretend to be trees. "The dog will come around and sniff your hands to identify who you are, because dogs learn through scent," she told the children. This led to a discussion of how to approach a strange dog by holding out the back of the hand to be sniffed, and the caution never to run from a dog because that could trigger a prey reaction.

To encourage social behavior, Lana produced a "magic" rope, which she hooked to the D ring on Grizzly's harness—a cotton rope instead of nylon or hemp so that if it slipped through a child's hand it would not cause a friction burn. The rope had clips on both ends that could be fastened to Grizzly's harness like reins and as many as three children on each side could hold on to it. "This is a sharing rope," Lana told the children. "All of you are going to take Grizzly for a walk, and you have to work together to get Grizzly to go left, right, forward, stop, stay, find something—whatever you decide." Other times she asked them to choose a leader to make the decisions, and occasionally she had them go for a walk with Grizzly one at a time. Whether it was a single child or several, Lana herself always had control of the dog via a short lead attached to his collar.

As she had done at other facilities, once the program at the halfway house was under way and it was clear what the needs were and how best TGSA could function to meet them, Lana turned the program over to other volunteers to carry on. Always it was Lana's goal to work herself out of a job. She would open up a program initially by first holding one or two meetings with the staff at a facility to discuss how staff and volunteers might work together. During these meetings she placed particular emphasis on the therapists' responsibility to communicate their goals for the clients and the handlers' ultimate say over what the animals could and could not do. She then worked out techniques to meet the goals, coached the handlers, and gave further on-the-job training as it became apparent how various scenarios played out. When the program was up and running, she moved on to repeat the steps at another facility.

It was important for the TGSA handlers to feel comfortable with a facility and the people working there. Lana opened up one facility only to pull out when the handlers reported several occasions when the patients did not receive sufficient care. For instance, a patient urinated in one session and no one bothered to clean up, an indifference that appeared characteristic of the general treatment of the patients. In another setting, she encountered an obnoxious, raunchy therapist and immediately went to the director to voice her concern and say that volunteers could not be asked to work with such a man.

When a program was up and running, a particular handler might experience a personality conflict with the therapist. In that case the handler was changed, but only once; if the problem persisted, TGSA withdrew from the facility. From experience, Lana learned the importance of including all personnel who would be working in the AAT program in the initial assessment. This educated the staff about working with the AAT teams, while at the same time giving Lana an opportunity to judge how supportive of AAT the staff members were; there were instances where the administration wanted to try animal-assisted therapy but the therapists themselves were cool to the idea.

In acute-care facilities, the patient turnover tended to be high and it was rare for a therapy team of handler and animal to see the same patient for more than three visits. The opposite was true in rehabilitation programs, where treatment was usually a long-term affair and the volunteers were expected to stay the distance until the patient was released, transferred, had a status change, or died. In such instances, co-treating was common; that is, two handlers and two dogs worked with the client so that if one team fell ill or went on vacation, the other could continue the therapy without interruption.

Co-treatment was, however, not feasible in psychiatric settings because of the confidentiality of the material and because it often took a very long time to establish a relationship with the client. Indeed, it was likely not to be possible to establish a relationship at all if two handlers were present in addition to the therapist. Lana would assess the needs initially and then designate another handler to carry on.

This was her plan when the possibility of using long-term animal-assisted therapy at a residential treatment center for emotionally disturbed children came up. All twenty-four children at the center had been in several placements and their behavior was extreme. To test whether animal-assisted therapy could be of any value with such children, it was decided to try a pilot project with just one child. Two children with severe attachment disorder were the most likely candidates, and since one, Cynthia, had both a mother and grandmother who visited her, the other girl, Arden, who had no one, was chosen.

Arden had a history of neglect, abandonment, and abuse, her therapist, Mark, told Lana. She had been taken from her family and placed in a foster home when she was six because she was being physically and sexually abused. Then her family made whatever changes were necessary to get her back and Arden was returned to them, abused again, and removed again. This happened repeatedly, so that by the time Arden was twelve years old, she had been in thirteen foster homes. "What's sad with kids like this," Mark told Lana, "is that you have to build a case against the parents to be able to get the kids somewhere they're safe, and if you can't make the case stick, the kids ride a merry-go-round of being abused, being safe, and being abused, gaining and losing homes and families. They learn not to give out information, not to trust, not to invest a lot in people as a way of protecting themselves."

Arden, Mark said, had extreme difficulty in trusting anyone and forming any sort of attachment. She was expert at distancing people, at keeping herself isolated from them, which meant that therapy so far had been ineffective. His hope was that bringing an animal into the treatment program might create an opportunity for her to receive unconditional acceptance and nurturing. He looked down at Grizzly, who was lying beside Lana's chair. "A dog like this would be perfect," Mark said hopefully. "I'm really impressed with his calmness and willingness to just let people be around him."

"It can be Grizzly," Lana said. "Grizzly and me."

"Then I have to ask whether, no matter what, you will stick it out with Arden, either until we see it's not working or until she leaves the program. This little girl has to have something she can hook into, really hold on to, without any worry about losing it."

"That's why it's going to be me, because I'm the only one I can make that sort of commitment for."

"Good. We're in this together then."

A day and time for the first session was set, and Lana and Grizzly were in the therapy room, Grizzly resting with his head on his paws and Lana sitting on the floor beside him, when Mark came in with Arden.

The girl was taller than Lana had expected, with skinny legs and grimy knees, bitten fingernails and bony elbows. Her hair, a nondescript shade lurking drably between blond and brown, was short and stringy and oddly bunched. Her eyes looked everywhere but at Lana and slid over and past Grizzly without a flicker of interest. She joined Mark and Lana on the floor at Mark's insistence but answered none of his questions and gazed at objects around the room when Lana, to help Mark out, began speaking of Grizzly.

Lana reminded herself that this totally unresponsive child was surely frightened and hurting inside, but that did not make it any easier to deal with someone who would not talk and pretended not to hear. The girl reached for a rag doll lying near and began to dig a finger into it to enlarge a tiny hole and pull out the stuffing. When Mark commented on what she was doing, Arden threw the doll in a corner, scrambled to her feet, and roamed about the room, picking up objects and slamming them down again.

Grizzly's head lifted and he turned in one direction, then another, as though looking from one to another person, but since he could not see, Lana surmised he was trying to glean information about the situation through his senses of smell and hearing. Apparently he reached a conclusion, for with no signal from Lana, he stood up and slowly moved out into a shadowed hallway. Arden, her attention finally caught, watched him go. Grizzly settled in a dark patch and began his style of talk, making chirking sounds deep in his throat.

For the first time Arden looked full at Lana. "What's he doing?" she demanded.

"I don't know."

"What's he saying?"

"It sounds to me like he wants you to go over there."

"What for?"

"To be with him, I guess."

"That's silly." Arden snatched up the rag doll and thumped it repeatedly on the side of a table. But the thumping slowed; she was listening again. Slowly, as if Grizzly's voice were a thread drawing the girl to him, Arden moved toward the hallway. Lana held her breath. Would this child, the recipient of so much abuse and notorious in the residence for not being able to keep her hands to herself, turn the abuse on the dog? Grizzly woofled beguilingly. Arden was standing over him now. She stared at him but did not touch him. After a while she drifted down beside him. Grizzly's voice turned low and questioning. Arden began to talk, and at the end of each sentence Grizzly made sounds of understanding. Arden confided that she couldn't get along with the other kids and no one liked her, that she hit the kids and took things that belonged to them, that she was ugly and lonely. Did she know that Mark and Lana were listening? Did she want them to hear her so they would find ways to help her? Mark and Lana wondered—and silently blessed Grizzly for keeping the session from being a total waste.

Grizzly's visits to Arden were set at two weeks apart rather than weekly to give them a special quality and to have Arden know that she had to put work in on her therapy on her own, that

Grizzly would not always be present to be a go-between. Because Arden's personal care skills were so poor, Lana brought Grizzly's brush to a session and talked to Arden about the care animals had to have. She explained the type of coat Grizzly had, and the two of them hunkered down on the floor and analyzed the two layers of hair. Lana described how Grizzly shed and how he was dependent on her to keep him comfortable and healthy by combing and brushing him every day.

At subsequent sessions, as a way of involving Arden with Grizzly and encouraging her to handle him in thoughtful ways, Lana brought all of Grizzly's grooming tools, dedandering spray, and moisturing lotions and taught Arden how to use them. Arden learned that Grizzly needed to have his teeth brushed and that, like a person, he needed to have his face washed, his ears cleaned, and his toenails clipped and filed. Arden listened intently and followed Lana's directions with such care that one day Lana brought Grizzly to a session "naked."

"We have to visit the hospital after we leave here, and I've done nothing to prepare him," Lana told Arden. "I'm leaving it all up to you."

Arden started at Grizzly's nose and worked her way to his tail, grooming him competently and completely, to his evident pleasure and her satisfaction. Lana and Mark hoped that the thorough dog grooming would affect Arden's own self-care, which to some extent it did, but this was to remain an on-and-off matter for a very long time. When she had first come to the residential treatment home, Arden had been much, much too organized, with every piece of clothing folded to the same size and stacked precisely. Then she went to the other extreme and the staff had to remove her clothes from her room to keep her from ripping them to shreds. There was a similar problem with her hair; when Arden became angry or anxious, she pulled her hair out in clumps, making for a strange assortment of bald spots and areas of varying lengths. Now, with the care she was giving Grizzly, she was at least conscious that her hair deserved better treatment and she yanked at it and twisted it in her fingers with far less vehemence.

Brushing Grizzly, ostensibly directing all her attention to him, enabled Arden to lower her defenses and communicate better with Mark and Lana. She had somewhere to look and something to occupy her hands while they talked, and if the talk became too upsetting, she could always bury her face against Grizzly and be comforted. Arden came to know every knuckle, every bump, every bone and muscle of Grizzly's body, while Grizzly so came to trust her that when he had a broken molar she was the only one he would allow to look at it. For some part of the session in which he was suffering from toothache, she kept handling him and he made no objection, but finally she realized that he really did not feel well and would be better off without her mauling him. She lay down beside him with her head next to his head, and both of them fell asleep.

After the session, Mark said to Lana that he would not have believed it. "This is a kid who is *hyper*sensitive to everything that is going on around her, and here she is falling asleep with two other people in the room."

Mark had commented in the course of the session that it was his experience with animals that when they did not feel well, they did not want anyone touching them. Here was Grizzly, he pointed out, accepting Arden's handling without complaint, which suggested how much he cared about her. This experience and one other convinced Arden that she and Grizzly had a true friendship.

It happened on a day when Arden had to have some blood drawn for medical purposes and had reacted with a terrific tantrum. Mark started the session by telling Arden he was angry about her outburst, that he felt she was taking advantage and manipulating the staff instead of cooperating with them. "If it happens again when Grizzly is scheduled to visit," he warned, "I'll call Lana and cancel the visit." As he continued to discuss how everyone, including Grizzly, had rules to follow, Grizzly put his nose in Arden's hand and began to woofle, softly at first but then more insistently. He seemed to be saying, *Hey, I don't want to lose our visits*, which Lana confirmed by describing how Grizzly began saying, *Woo-woo-woo* and snapping his teeth to urge her to hurry when the car made the turn that told Grizzly they were going to the residence.

Grizzly, with Lana's cooperation, had given Arden a necklace with a red heart bearing Grizzly's name. Usually Arden had it tucked away in her room, but there were days she carried it with her and Mark knew it was a sign that she was having a tough time and needed something to hold on to. In individual therapy with her, Mark often referred back to Griz, saying, "You're having a problem with this kid. If the kid were Griz, how would you handle it?" Objectifying the problem and putting it in terms of a creature she loved enabled Arden to step back and work through the steps that would solve the problem.

"It's a great prompt, one I use all the time," Mark told Lana in a debriefing session. "I build on her relationship with Griz by saying, 'Look at what you've done. You've built a real friendship with Griz. Now let's take that one step further and see how you can build relationships with people.'"

Arden had many bad days and weeks and suffered through many and many a setback because she was, in Mark's words, the most impulsive kid he had ever worked with in his twenty years of experience. "The slightest thing can set her off," Mark told Lana. "Usually we're pretty good at picking out what triggers a kid, but sometimes we're shaking our heads and saying why now? She's having this great day, and suddenly she's off and going down, really anxious, really nervous, really impulsive. But then Griz comes, and this hyper, wired kid mellows out and becomes as calm as he is."

Because the pilot project with Arden was showing how useful animal-assisted therapy could be, another handler and her dog were assigned to a boy at the residential center for what also promised to be long-term therapy. When making assignments, Lana stressed that volunteers working with abused children had to commit themselves to regular visits that might go on as long as three years, because such children needed the experience of having reliable adults in their lives. If such a commitment was impossible or if the volunteer preferred work with a different type of problem, there were other facilities and other patients who needed them.

Grace Whitaker and Moose, one of her Labradors, were regular visitors at a school for children with multiple disabilities. The goals for the children might be as simple as learning to pet the dog with an open hand rather than a closed fist or the more complicated task of learning to give the dog hand signals. Some of the children talked very little, some not at all; the handlers kept repeating commands for them to give the dog and were occasionally rewarded by a child mouthing the words on his own. Despite the possibility of being struck or fallen against by a child with poor motor control, Moose never reacted aggressively. He seemed to understand the limitations of the children. He knew they needed him, and he was never anything but patient with them and eager for return visits.

In an almost uncanny fashion, all the dogs appeared to understand the responsibility of being therapy dogs. For instance, Paulette Bethel with Onyx and Cheryl Weaver with Megan were working at a residential facility for children two to six years old. Two aides and seven children were in the room with them when a four-year-old decided to climb a bookcase. As an aide pulled the child off, the bookcase swayed and crashed not six inches away from where Megan lay with a child resting against her. Had she leaped to her feet, the child would have been thrown into the path of the bookcase. As it was, the dog neither moved nor flinched.

A little boy in that same residential center had a tonsillectomy. He was in such pain that he refused to swallow food or medicine despite the pleadings of the staff. All he wanted, he whispered, was to see Megan. The message was relayed to Cheryl, who arrived with Megan and a popsicle. Megan climbed up on the bed with the little boy, the popsicle was divided, and as Megan licked away at her share, the little boy followed suit with his.

Another success was accomplished by a gifted handler named Janet McFadden, who visited with her dog Brandi at a facility for blind children. A little girl who was partially sighted screamed whenever there was anything unfamiliar in the room and was particularly terrified of the dog. The goal set for animal-assisted therapy was to attempt to desensitize her to the strange and foreign. Janet and her yellow Lab sat seven feet away while the therapist held the little girl in her lap and comforted her. In utter silence, Janet and the dog inched forward; in fifteen minutes they were five feet away from the child; after half an hour, they were a foot away. When they were inches away, the child began to scream. Janet casually lay down on her stomach, as flat on the floor as the dog.

"Would you like to hold Brandi's leash?" she said, offering it to the child, who snatched at it and pulled her hand back. Gently soothing her with her voice, Janet took off the little girl's shoes and socks while the dog lay motionless. "Brandi's fur is like velvet." Janet crooned. "It's probably as soft as anything you've ever felt. You tell me if it is." She smoothed the little girl's feet over the dog's coat. The child smiled; she liked the feel. After a while the child reached out to touch the dog with her hand. That proved safe and interesting. She moved off the therapist's lap to Brandi's side, and Brandi gave her hand a bit of a lick in greeting. The little girl giggled. She was never so afraid of strange shadows in her dim world again.

Children who were deaf as well as blind attended a special school, but for children like this little girl with vision problems alone, classrooms had been set aside in a regular elementary school. Handlers and dogs visited the classrooms to acquaint the children with the animals and show that they could be helpful. The children had to learn to use a white guide stick to help them get around. Since it was difficult for them to use the stick and keep their balance at the same time, they liked having a large dog alongside to lean against. A boy named Barry, who was particularly timid about venturing forth, had Grizzly as his guide dog one day and was walking down a long hall with him. Lana was on Grizzly's other side, next to the wall, and they were halfway down the hall, doing nicely, when suddenly the double doors at the end exploded open, loosing a horde of running, shouting children upon them. Grizzly quickly angled to put his own body between the rampaging children and the boy.

The boy started to whimper. "What'll I do? I'm scared."

Lana, who was herself frightened they would be bowled over, said, "You tell these kids that this is your guide dog and he's working and they can't touch him."

The kids were grabbing at Grizzly, who paid no attention. "This is my guide dog," Barry whispered. "You can't touch him." He said it again and again, his voice getting more confident with each repetition. Teachers came through the double doors and the flood of students drained off into classrooms, and Lana and Barry and Grizzly were alone.

"You handled that well, Barry, really well," Lana told the boy.

"I was sort of scared," he admitted.

"Of course. So was I. But you did fine," she said, and noted the squareness of Barry's shoulders, the lift of his head, as he ordered Grizzly to turn and guide him back to the classroom.

Dealing with handicapped children is not an easy assignment for an inexperienced handler, and Karen Schroyer admitted she was almost sick with nervousness when she first took her Australian shepherd Hawkeye to visit children with cerebral palsy. The five children in the room were lying on the floor when she and Hawkeye entered, and she worried that, as active and vocal as Hawkeye was, he might inadvertently bring harm to them. They sat down on the floor next to a three-year-old girl with multiple disabilities, and the therapist braced the little girl and guided her hand to stroke Hawkeye. When his handsome tail was used to tickle her face, the girl managed the slightest of smiles. The therapist wanted to have more stimulation on the child's face, so Karen placed a treat on her cheek, praying that Hawkeye would wait patiently, which he did until Karen gave the command. Then he retrieved it neatly, and just for a moment a light came into the little girl's eyes.

"Hawkeye and I have had our good days and our great days working in animal-assisted therapy," Karen says. "I still get butterflies in my stomach before a visit, but Hawkeye handles visits like an old pro. In the past year, at a residential treatment center, he has made fast friends with an eight-year-old boy. Steven has learned to take care of Hawkeye, brushing his coat and his teeth, and he plays with him, confides in him, and absolutely loves Hawkeye completely, this in a boy who has a history of animal abuse."

Another of the venues in which TGSA established a program was at the state mental hospital. They were asked to work with adolescent female patients who had a variety of disorders—manic depression, anorexia, post-traumatic stress syndrome—to test whether therapy animals could make a difference in the girls' behavior toward one another and in their self-care and whether, by giving commands to the dogs, the girls would become more self-assertive. It was also hoped that with the dogs present to take some of the attention off the girls, the girls might become more able and willing to talk about why they were in the hospital and what they could do to make changes in their behavior.

One of the teams coming in to work with the girls was Grace Whitaker, who, in addition to her two Labradors, had acquired a miniature pinscher named Raisin, a tiny male weighing only a few pounds. To Grace's mortification, when a shy, unassertive girl held Raisin, he immediately began humping the girl's arm. Pelvic thrusting in dogs is a way of trying to show dominance, but these girls knew little or nothing about canine behavior, and since many had been sexually molested, they knew only one interpretation of the action. Grace Whitaker had every intention of immediately replacing Raisin with Moose, one of her Labradors, but the therapist suggested that instead they try to turn this negative behavior into a positive.

At the next session the therapist asked the girls how they felt about Raisin's inappropriate behavior. They could relate to that and the comments, which came thick and fast, were revealing of the girls' own attitudes. Next, the therapist asked what could be done to help the dog. The first step, she suggested, was to analyze why Raisin was doing what he was doing. The smallest girl in the group hazarded a guess that perhaps because the dog was so little, he had to act big and tough. The biggest and toughest girl in the group said no, it was because inside he was afraid. The discussion that ensued was the most fruitful that had yet occurred in this group of highly defensive girls. At a later meeting, the therapist prompted the girls not just to identify Raisin's behavior but to come up with ways of modifying it by saying no and directing him to something positive to do, like playing ball, and then rewarding him with a treat when he behaved appropriately.

Using a dog's shortcomings as a subtle mentoring tool worked so well that Lana brought Kodyella, who was afraid of other dogs, into the group to show that even a large German shepherd, so self-possessed on the outside, could be frightened on the inside. With Lana's reassurance and support, Kodyella stayed and interacted with the group despite the presence of other dogs, illustrating to the girls that just because you are afraid of something doesn't mean you can't do it, especially if you get a bit of support.

So successful was animal-assisted therapy with these adolescents that the girls were given passes to attend a large dog show to help man The Good Shepherd Association booth. The booth was designed to attract more dog owners to join the organization, for as fast as volunteers were trained, more calls came in asking for their services. The Good Shepherd Association was Utah's only organization offering animal-assisted therapy at that time, and learning, rehabilitation, hospital, and residential treatment centers were eager to schedule sessions. Lana had more than proven her hunch that loving animals can create a connection with people that human beings are incapable of. Now the problem was how to keep up with the need.

10
Animal-Assisted Therapy

People who were interested in taking part in the work The Good Shepherd Association was doing but who did not have a suitable animal often resolved to acquire a puppy and sought Paulette or Lana's advice on how to go about training it.

Training starts, they were told, the minute a puppy is brought home at eight to ten weeks of age. Bonding with human beings is essential, so the puppy must live in the house with his person or people, not in a kennel outside. Socializing is further accomplished by taking the puppy out in company in as many different circumstances as possible; for instance, by taking him to the park and for walks in the neighborhood. Because the puppy needs to get along with other dogs, the more he is able to be around them and play with them, the better, and because he also needs to get along with children, the same is true of them.

Paulette's suggestion was this: "If the children in your area will help, see if you can expose your pup to lots of little people. To dogs, children are a different species from adults, and frequently the quickness and noise of playing children can trigger a 'prey' drive in your dog that will limit the dog's ability to be used in a therapeutic setting with children later. Early imprinting with running, yelling kids can make a difference as to whether or not you can later take your dog into a children's residential setting or hospital."

In general, on Ella Brown's suggestion, Lana recommended the training techniques described by the monks of New Skete. The monks raise German shepherds at their monastery in New York State and have written two books about schooling puppies in ways that insure they will grow up to be responsible dogs and great animals to live with. The monks direct that puppies should learn to lie still by being lightly held down. This teaches them that the person is in charge; they do not have to be afraid, but they do have to do what they are told. To get puppies used to being held and handled, they can be cuddled in a lap, both right side up and upside down, and their toes and ears and mouth handled until they are densitized to being touched on any part of the body. Pressure training starts light and is very gradually increased; the dogs are praised and told they are good. The same thing is accomplished by having puppies lie down and roll over, with lots of massaging done while they are on the floor. This teaches them that handling is not something to be afraid of, that nothing bad is going to happen.

For their own pleasure and to give them exercise, dogs should be taught to fetch, play ball, and catch. For therapy work it is useful if the dog is taught to take a treat without snapping at it. This is done by having the treat in your hand with only about half an inch of it visible. You bring it up to the dog's nose and say, "Take it," and when the dog snaps at it, you say "Ouch!" For some dogs, hearing that is enough, but if it is not, you quickly move your hand out of reach, saying, "Ouch, ouch, ouch!" Eventually the dog will stop and think and begin to slow down, and you continue working until he or she takes it really slowly and then learns to take it from your lips without touching you.

During the first year, dogs are of course house-trained and schooled to have good manners. They learn to walk on a loose lead without pulling and to heed commands. They learn the meaning of "Off" and "Leave it." "Leave it" is for when the dog is about to do something you don't want. It orders him to stop, to keep his mouth off it, to leave it alone. It is also used to tell the dog to stop barking. When Kodyella and Grizzly are barking like crazy in the house, Lana goes to them and says, "You're doing your job, that's good, but now it's time to stop," and if that does not work, she says emphatically, "Leave it!" Never does she strike the dogs. "I don't need to spank them, and I never would. If you're using positive reinforcement, they're going to want to do what's right. They want to please you. If they know you're unhappy, they'll want to stop, and with positive reinforcement you can redirect their behavior."

In order for dogs to become certified as therapy animals through the Delta Society, a veterinarian must attest to their good health and then they must go through the Delta Society's Pet-Partners evaluation to establish their skills and aptitude. The examiner tests the dogs' obedience training, whether they are well-behaved, friendly, and enjoy being around people, how they react to unfamiliar sights and sounds, how startled they are by sudden or loud noises, and how they react to pressure on various parts of the body.

If a dog passed the Pet-Partners evaluation and the owner wished to become a TGSA handler, both were required to undergo the eight weeks of TGSA training. With graduation from the training, both dog and handler were provided with Pet Partners and TGSA identification tags to be worn whenever they were working. Dogs had to have a short lead, not a long or flexible lead that would allow the dog to get out ahead of the handler, and a harness that fit snugly so that it did not slip if a child walking with the dog was holding on to it. A gym bag or backpack was another piece of recommended equipment since it could hold a portable water bowl for the dog, treats, toys, balls, grooming tools, and anything else that might be needed in a therapy session.

Because therapy is hard work for the dogs, the rule about not working them for more than an hour at a time was firm, along with providing eight to ten hours of rest between working sessions. Also emphasized was exercise time for the dogs to maintain them at their proper weight and reduce stress. There is considerable benefit to a dog in playing ball, going for a walk or run in the park, or being taken somewhere to play with other dogs after being engaged in therapy work. Activity provides the dog with physical and mental release. The owner can also give back to the animal some of the emotional healing the dog provides for others by spending quiet time with the dog, talking gently, massaging and kneading the dog's muscles, and giving ear rubs by lightly stroking the animal's ears.

Without exception, TGSA handlers reported a change in their therapy dog's demeanor when the gear bag came out and the collar and harness went on. The dogs knew they were going to work and were responsive, well-behaved, and self-assured. This was business and they took it seriously. Betty Brown reported that her nine-year-old yellow Labrador, Sam, "seems to know what days he is going to work as soon as he wakes up on those mornings, and he never lets me out of his sight until we are ready to go. He sits extremely still while I am putting his harness on him, but then he gathers his leash in his mouth and bounds out to the car and dances around it, waiting to get in and go." She then added: "Anyone who says these dogs don't understand what they are doing or believe that they are not doing real work has not watched the excitement it gives Sam and the undivided attention he gives to the clients he works with."

A heartwarming experience happened to Grace Whitaker, who described it in these words: "To me, there's no greater payoff for volunteering than seeing a miracle happen before your eyes, and I cashed in big last month at a facility for disabled children where Moose and I volunteer. For six months Moose has been helping a spunky little girl who has multiple disabilities use a walker, motivating her to walk farther and faster. Then a month ago her teacher said, 'I know Ginnie's strong enough to walk without the walker. I wonder if she'd do it with just Moose by her side.' The teacher took Ginnie out of her walker and stood her up next to Moose. She put the handle from Moose's harness in Ginnie's left hand and held her right hand. I was on the other side of Moose with my traffic lead on his collar. When Ginnie signed Forward, the four of us went down the hall. *For the first time in her life, Ginnie walked without an apparatus!* You can't pay for the privilege of witnessing a moment like that. Moose helped a miracle happen for Ginnie that day, and I was there to see it—not Ginnie's family, just her teacher, my dog, and me."

An advantage of having animals work with people with physical disabilities is that animals are calming and encouraging, often motivating people to do things they do not want to do or believe they cannot do. On one occasion, Lana, having made this point to a group of volunteers in training at a rehabilitation hospital, took the volunteers across the hall to show them the physical therapy room and the types of apparatus used with the patients. At the far side of the room was a woman in a wheelchair, crying. A physical therapist was saying to her, "Ruthie, come on, please try this. You can go back to your room as soon as you've done this exercise," and the woman was moaning in protest, "I can't. It hurts. It hurts."

Lana saw that Grizzly's attention had been caught and he was eager to go to the woman. She said to the volunteers, "Let me go over there with Griz, and perhaps you'll see what I've been talking about. The therapist is trying to get the woman to move her right arm on that device and she is crying; she doesn't want to do it because it's too painful, so let's see what Griz does."

Lana approached with Grizzly and asked the therapist if Grizzly might say hello. The therapist, with a relieved look, said, "Oh, yes, absolutely." The patient had been so focused on her painful arm that she had not seen Grizzly, but now she broke into a big smile. "Oh, what a gorgeous dog!" Grizzly poked his nose under the damaged arm, moved his head until it was under her hand, and encouraged her to move her arm up and down through his gentle nudges, all the while talking with brisk encouragement in his throat. The woman laughed with delight, said, "This is wonderful!", and the arm that was too painful to move went up and down faster and faster until the therapist said, "Okay, Ruthie, you're done. You've made your quota."

Lana returned to her students and reminded them that earlier she had referred to studies in which animals had been used to distract patients from pain. "And now you've seen it for yourselves," she said. She went on to tell them about a patient named Lucinda, a twenty-two-year-old woman studying veterinary medicine, who had been on her way to get married in Arizona when a drunken driver ran into her car head on, breaking almost every bone in Lucinda's body; her skull, jaw, pelvis, arms, and legs were crushed. In the hospital her teeth were wired shut, and she was totally immobilized except for one hand. She was in tremendous pain and cried and cried and cried. In desperation, the hospital asked Lana to visit with Grizzly. "There's nothing more we can do for her physically," they told Lana. "Her heart is breaking and she is all but destroyed emotionally, which is probably why the pain medication isn't working for her. If we could just get her emotions stabilized, maybe we could get the pain under control."

A physical therapist led Lana to Lucinda's room. The young woman, who could not sit up, was in a reclining chair packed around with pillows, and tears were streaming down her face. Grizzly and Lana moved closer to her, and Lana said, "Hi, I have a friend here. Would you like to visit with Grizzly?" Grizzly came up underneath Lucinda's hand and nuzzled it.

"What's that?" Lucinda whispered through her wired teeth.

"This is Grizzly," Lana told her, and Grizzly confirmed it with his own brand of talk. "He's saying hello. Let me get him closer so you can see him better." Lana pulled a chair up and Grizzly climbed on it and sat down, his head now a bit higher than Lucinda's so she could look in his eyes while he talked to her, which seemed to please her. But then Lucinda went into spasm and began screaming in agony. It was nightmarish to hear, and Lana, hoping the therapist would say yes, asked if she and Grizzly should go away.

"There's nothing we can do. We can't give her any more drugs. Keep talking to her."

"Okay," Lana said doubtfully. She signaled to Grizzly to stay where he was and told Lucinda that they were going for a walk with Grizzly. "Yes, you can," she answered the look in Lucinda's eyes. "Close your eyes and let's go. Tell Grizzly in your mind to lead you on a path through sand dunes. The wind is rippling the dune grass, the sun is warm, the sky is very blue with small white puffs of clouds. Grizzly leads you over a rise, and there is the ocean with the sun glinting on the waves. You and Grizzly run across the white sand to the water's edge. Grizzly's talking to you. Can you hear him?" Grizzly all along had been counterpointing Lana's voice with his own small talk. "He's telling you to kick off your shoes and go wading with him."

By the end of the adventure in which Lucinda and Grizzly watched tiny crabs scuttling into holes, found a whorled shell with the sound of the sea in it, had a picnic and fed the leftovers to a bold seagull, Lucinda's tears had stopped and her pain had eased. When Lana saw how much she and Grizzly had helped Lucinda, they visited often after that. Lucinda looked forward to being with Grizzly because it was clear he cared about her by how eagerly he responded to her and divined what she was saying through her clenched teeth, whether it was, "Grizzly, sit," or "Grizzly, let's go for a walk."

When she got a bit better, Grizzly pulled her wheelchair and participated in her physical therapy sessions, bringing her a rubber bone in his mouth and then backing up when she reached for it so she had to take a step toward him. *Come and get me,* he seemed to be taunting her. Later it was a ball he made her come after, and when she threw it for him, he deliberately ran in the wrong direction so she had to speak to tell him, "Grizzly, no, it's over there." And again the wrong direction, and again, making her speak and also making her laugh because he was clearly clowning. Then he'd snap up the ball, bring it to her, wait for her to throw it and say, "Go get it, Griz!"—and do nothing, until suddenly he'd run directly to it and bring it back rapidly, making her laugh again at his duplicity.

A year later Lucinda had learned to walk again, haltingly but on her own. She still had many plastic surgeries ahead of her and she called herself a bionic woman because of the metal rods holding her bones together, but she was alive and out of pain and the tears were long gone. The poignancy of a lovely young woman on

Lana and Grizzly reporting for hospital rounds in 1992. This was when Lana would begin to learn of Grizzly's unique healing and intuitive abilities.

photo by JayLynn Studios

Lana and Grizzly in 1994, while Lana was executive director of The Good Shepherd Association.

Grizzly in 1995, resting at home after a therapy session, enjoying the smells and sounds only dogs appreciate.

Kodyella and Grizzly share muzzle kisses, a morning ritual.

Grizzly working with a child with multiple disabilities, providing sensory stimulus administered with love. This is what Grizzly does best, as reflected in the boy's face. Grizzly is crooning, making little soft woofing noises that only the child can hear.

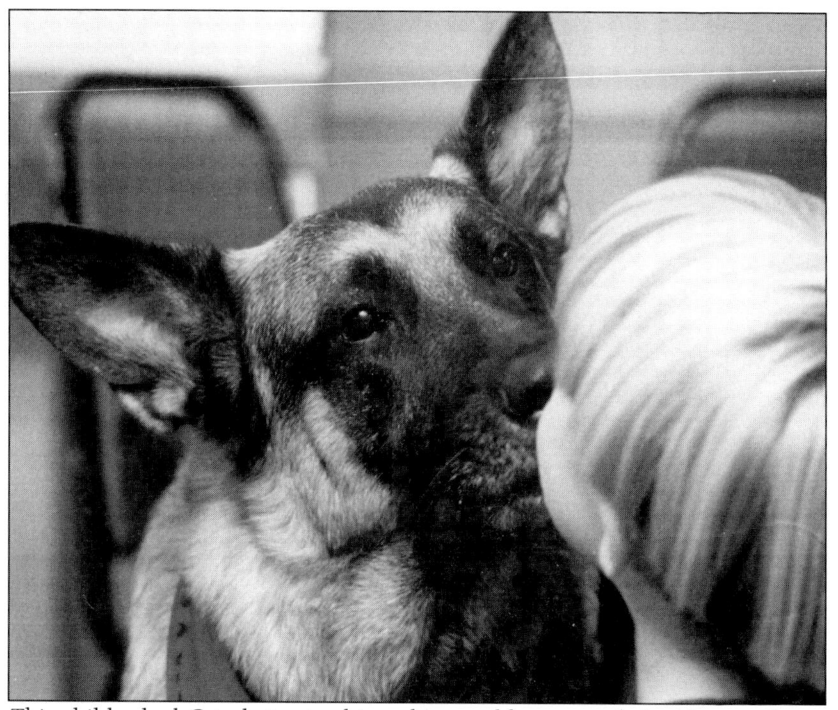

This child asked Grizzly to give him a kiss, and he responded with a gentle nuzzle. This exercise, a big dog listening and following a request, is empowering to a child.

Lana and Grizzly with Betty Brown, executive director of the Utah Animal-Assisted Therapy Association, and her yellow Lab, Sam, meeting Utah governor Mike Leavitt during a conference of hospice providers in the fall of 1997.

A group shot before the handlers go on assignment: Jolene Lofy with Alex, Grace Whitaker with Snickers, Lana with Grizzly, Betty Brown with Sam, and Mara Ulis with Elvis.

photo by Carl J. Widmer

Judy Mills and Cody. Cody and Grizzly co-treated an emotionally troubled child for a year with impressive results.

Debbie Nozawa and her sheltie, Cassi, with a special needs student at the Oakridge School in Provo, Utah. In this photo, they are doing animal-assisted physical therapy, encouraging the boy to sit up.

Debbie and Cassi encouraging a child to walk a little farther. A physical therapist is standing behind the child.

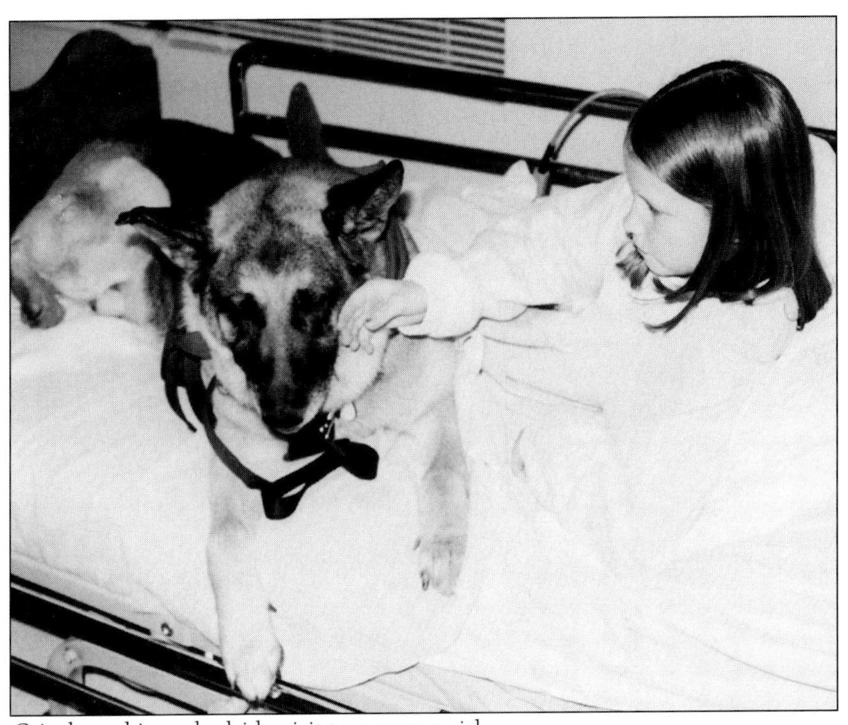

Grizzly making a bedside visit to a young girl.

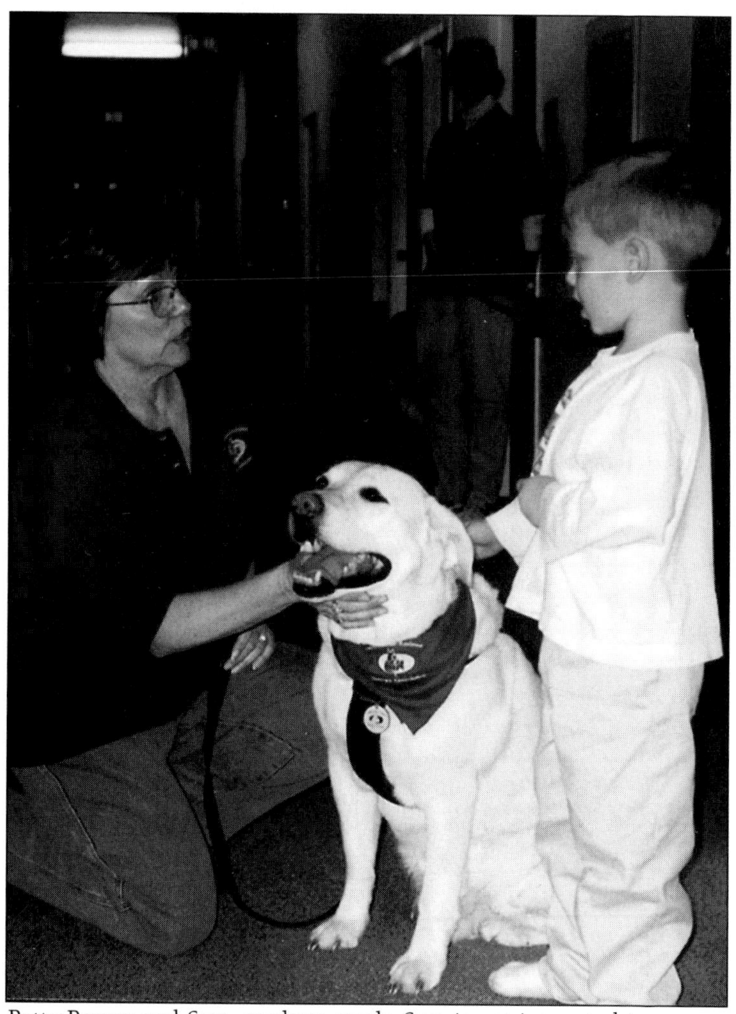

Betty Brown and Sam, ready to work. Sam is not interested in looking at the camera because he has already spotted his client and wants to get started. Like the other dogs, when his harness goes on, he knows what he is supposed to do and is ready to go.

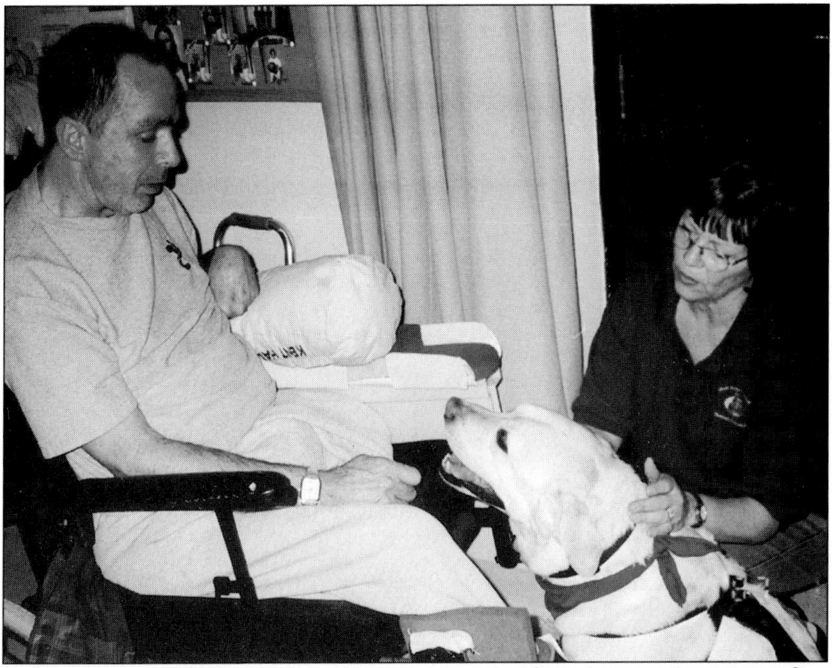

Betty and Sam with a patient. Visits like these significantly raise the spirits of many institutionalized people, increasing their willingness to participate in therapy and social activities as well, even when the animals are not present.

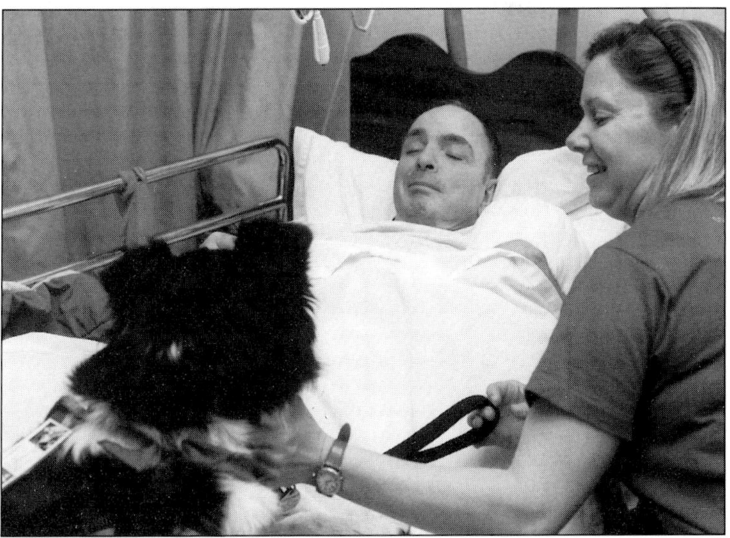

Karen Schroyer and Hawkeye visit a patient. Hawkeye encourages patients confined to bed to stretch and even talk.

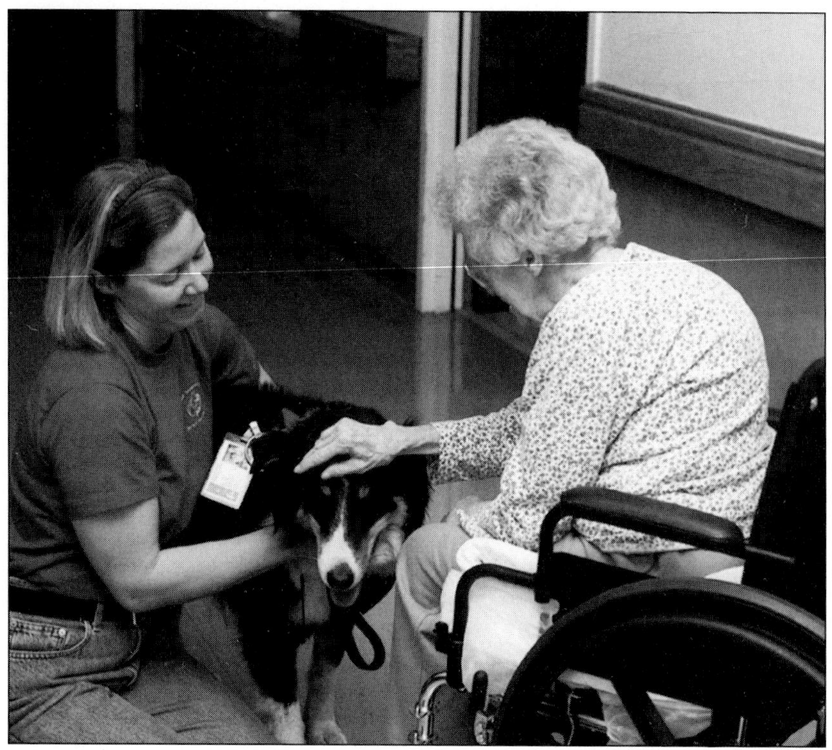

Karen Schroyer and Hawkeye greet a patient. Many patients look forward to these visits eagerly, which stimulate them to come out of their rooms and interact with others.

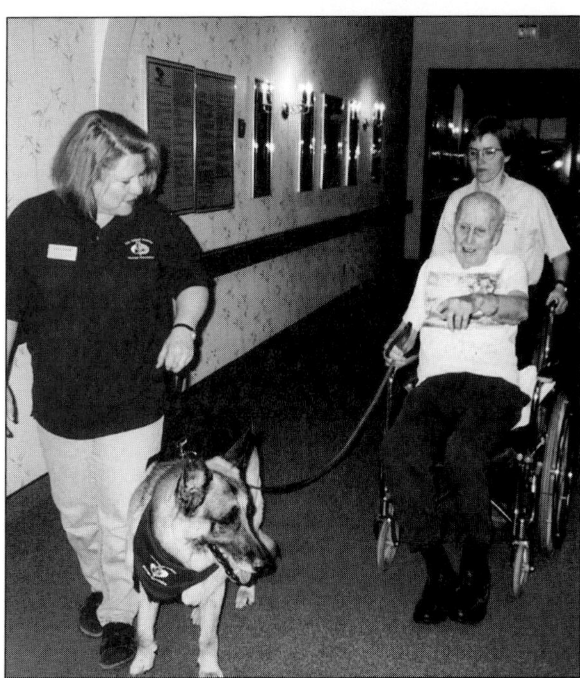

Lana and Grizzly going for a walk with a patient down a hospital corridor. During wheelchair walks, patients are given a lead and are encouraged to give the dog commands, while the handler maintains actual control of the animal through a short lead such as the one Lana is holding. Note that a professional staff member accompanies these walks and controls the wheelchair at all times.

Betty Brown, Sam, and patient. Reaching out to pet or brush the dog provides motivation to meet physical therapy goals.

photo by United Studios of America

Lana and Dave with Bayley, Grizzly, and Kodyella—a happy family!

her way to her wedding being so smashed had touched the public, and a television crew came to interview her about her relationship with Grizzly and how he had helped her get through the months of rehabilitation. "Grizzly's visits gave me something to look forward to. When he was with me, I wasn't in pain," Lucinda said. "It's like my pain went away and I could laugh. He teased me and talked to me and was such fun to be with."

Perhaps it was hearing how Grizzly helped Lucinda that prompted a caseworker to get in touch with Lana about another young woman who had been in a terrible accident that had left her unable to speak, to walk, or to use her left hand. After being hospitalized for months, Sophie, at age twenty, was placed in a nursing home. Three years later a caseworker took an interest in her and arranged to have her moved to a group home shared by five mentally retarded men. Unable to communicate except by spelling out every word or trying to sign with her only working hand, and able to move only to the extent of manipulating a lever on her wheelchair to position herself for television viewing, Sophie, not surprisingly, was given to bouts of rage at her fate. When the caseworker asked TGSA for help and mentioned that Sophie had trained her cocker spaniel to respond to some hand signals, Lana and Paulette decided they would ask Sophie to assist them in training their dogs to recognize hand signals, which would give them a legitimate excuse for visiting her.

To ensure that the first session would not end in frustration for Sophie because the dogs did not respond to her signals, Paulette brought her young Doberman, Testa Rosa, who already knew a few signals. Lana had intended to bring Kodyella because Grizzly's blindness would prevent him from seeing hand signals, but Grizzly was scheduled to be at a children's residence immediately after the session with Sophie. There would not be time to go home to get him so Lana brought him instead.

Testa Rosa and Paulette worked with Sophie for half an hour while Lana sat in a chair nearby and watched and Grizzly dozed at her feet. Then Sophie indicated that she wanted to see Grizzly because she had always had a fondness for German shepherds.

Lana took Grizzly to her and stood there talking with Paulette and the caseworker. Suddenly Grizzly gave out a loud bark, startling the three of them but producing a grin on Sophie's face. Lana asked Sophie what she had done and Sophie made a hand signal that Lana had never seen before and Grizzly could not see, but somehow the message to speak had gotten through to him. Sophie then put her arm beside Grizzly's shoulder and barely rubbed her thumb and middle finger together. Grizzly immediately lifted his paw and gave it to her to shake.

"You're unbelievable," Lana told him later, as she was placing the step stool he used to climb into the back of the van. "I can't explain how you do it, and I don't suppose you're going to tell me."

"Woof," said Grizzly.

"That's what I thought you'd say." She tugged his ear affectionately. "How'd you like to go see Arden now?"

"Woof, woof, woof!"

"Now you're talking!"

At the children's residential center, Arden and Mark were already in the meeting room when Lana and Grizzly arrived. In the doorway, Grizzly's head lifted sharply and Lana looked quickly from the therapist to the child, for it was palpable from the atmosphere in the room that something was wrong. Grizzly moved to Arden's side, and she put her arms around his neck.

"I don't have to stay five feet from Griz, do I?" Arden asked, sulky defiance in her voice.

Mark turned to Lana. "Arden's been having a bad day because a friend of hers—"

"My best friend," the girl interrupted.

"Your worst friend," Mark amended, and explained to Lana. "Her friend has been moved to another facility because he's been so disruptive here, and Arden's sad even though she shouldn't be because he cut a hole in her favorite sweater and hassled her and got her into trouble with the other kids and the staff."

"I liked him!"

"Why?"

"Because."

"Because he paid attention to you even if it was the wrong kind of attention? Nobody needs that kind of attention. All it does is make them a victim." He waited for Arden to reply, and when she did not, he explained to Lana, "She's on a five-foot rule, which means she can't get any closer than five feet to any other kid because she can't keep her hands to herself and she's pushing and grabbing kids' hats and shirts and flipping their ears."

As if to prove Mark right, Arden's hands were busily prowling through Grizzly's fur. Her head was down but her shoulders remained aggressively squared and their set suggested she did not intend to talk. Lana waited to be sure the dialogue was at an end and then spoke herself.

"Grizzly used to have a best friend named Nike. They played together every day for two years, and one day Grizzly took his best friend to visit a children's center with him because Nike was a search-and-rescue dog and the children wanted to meet him. The children decided it would be fun if one of them hid and the others told Nike to find him, so that's what they did, but it happened that Grizzly found the boy first. The boy was laughing and hugging Grizzly, and Nike came up and bit Grizzly's ear because he was mad that Grizzly got there before he did. Now, you know Grizzly is a fighter if he needs to be, but he was responsible for the little boy and he didn't move, he just dropped down.

"From that point on, Grizzly decided never to associate with Nike again even though Nike was sorry about what he'd done and wanted to go on playing with Grizzly in the fields like they always had. But Grizzly would have nothing to do with him. He chose to be alone rather than be a victim. And then Onyx came along, a beautiful Doberman, and they became friends. She loved to play ball and she taught Grizzly how. She would go after the ball and he would run beside her, and she'd drop the ball and let him have it.

"Sometimes we have to make choices. Grizzly didn't know he'd find another best friend, but he made the choice not to be a victim, which set him up for finding a new friend."

"Yeah," Arden said, and now her harsh voice had softened. "Yeah. Grizzly's smart."

"You're smart," Mark said.

Arden sprang up, snatched a yarn ball from a basket of toys, and tossed it into a corner. "Find it, Griz," she ordered. Grizzly did and brought the ball back to her. She whirled on Lana. "Where's his brush? I'm going to groom him."

"Hey, wait," Mark said. "Griz did what you told him to do. Pay him off. Give him a hug."

Afterward Mark said to Lana, "She's such a negatively inclined kid that it's still real hard for her to do something positive like giving Grizzly a hug."

"But did you see," Lana said, "that she gave me the beginning of a hug when Griz and I were leaving? It was awful quick, kind of furtive, but it was there."

"She's coming along, and I don't think she ever would have without Griz. We couldn't have reached her. Griz accepts her totally and she really trusts him."

"Would she make better progress if we came more often?"

"She'd love that, of course, but life isn't about having things be exactly like you wish. If she's going to make it in the outside world, she has to be able to control herself, she has to follow directions, she has to cooperate, she has to get along."

Lana looked up at him. "Will Arden make it?"

"I don't know," he said honestly. "I still don't know how much of a survivor she is." Then his tone changed. "If she does make it," he said, "a large part of it'll be because Griz has given her hope that there is something different out there than anything she's known before."

Because Grizzly was so specially suited to psychiatric work with children, Lana tended to designate other handlers to work in physical therapy settings. But one day the director of a rehabilitation hospital particularly asked her to bring Grizzly to the bedside of a retired physician who had been in a coma since falling from a tree weeks before. Lana could not imagine what a dog could do for someone in a coma, but the director urged her to come. "The man's wife says he loves dogs. If you don't mind, I'd just like to give it a try."

Lana was willing, and with the man's family looking on, she put Grizzly up on the bed, where he lay still against the body of the comatose man. After a while the dog gently nuzzled the man's hand. Next he did something Lana had never seen him do before, which was to lick the man's hand, gently and persistently. The man's wife never took her eyes off her husband, scanning for the smallest of signs. Suddenly she saw one. "Look! Look!" The man's fingers were moving in Grizzly's fur. He was responding to the feel of the dog.

After this initial stimulus, and following more visits from Grizzly, Dr. Bradley gradually regained consciousness. When he was fit enough for rehabilitation work to begin, Paulette and Onyx took over, spending an hour with him twice a week and working with him to regain as much use of his left side as possible. After each exhausting session, in which Dr. Bradley struggled to master the skills he would need if he was to return home, Onyx rewarded him by pulling his wheelchair for a cruise up and down the hospital corridors, an activity they both got a kick out of.

Then tragedy struck a second time. Dr. Bradley fell and once again he was in a coma. This time the struggle to come back was even harder and took even longer. Another handler and his black Labrador took over the animal-assisted therapy, and finally the valiant doctor was able to leave the hospital, at which point Paulette came back into the picture, this time in her guise as a dog trainer as she assisted Dr. Bradley and his wife with the training of a service dog to be Dr. Bradley's companion.

Although people do wake up from comatose states on their own, it was conceivable that it was Grizzly's warmth and weight, his breathing and heartbeat, wedged as he was almost the full length of Dr. Bradley's side, that made something in the doctor's brain stir into some degree of wakefulness. In any event, Lana was willing to try again when she was contacted about Jason, an eighteen-year-old with severe head injuries sustained when he was a passenger in a car returning from a school game. Jason, maintained on a respirator, was showing few signs of life and the staff could not justify keeping him in the hospital for extensive rehabilitative therapy unless a greater degree of response could be elicited.

"Ah, the dogs are here," a doctor said as Lana with Grizzly and Paulette with Testa Rosa entered the room. "Let's see if they can get Jason to open his eyes."

Grizzly was placed on the bed beside Jason. There was no reaction in the young man, but after a few minutes the monitors in the room registered a rise in his vital signs. His body was responding to stimuli; at some level he sensed the presence of the dog. Testa Rosa was placed on the bed against his other side, and the vital signs went still higher.

The dogs continued to visit, and other dogs and handlers took their turn. After four weeks, Jason's eyes were open and focusing, he was taken off the respirator, and the monitors were removed. Soon after that, he was able, with a great deal of help, to sit in a wheelchair and very slowly open his fingers to hold a dog biscuit. Getting the muscles in his hand to work took prolonged effort, but Jason kept at it without complaint until he could hold the biscuit out to the dog. When speech therapy got under way, Onyx was the dog who worked with him because her responses were very quick, which was rewarding to someone struggling to get words out. Jason's first spoken syllable was "On," an attempt to say the dog's name.

Rehabilitative therapy is arduous, often painful, and frequently discouraging, but when an animal is part of the therapy, the patient tends to focus on the animal and lose sight of the pain and effort. For instance, Jason, because his limbs were involuntarily curling up, needed to have weight on his legs, which was distressing and uncomfortable. But a ninety-five-pound dog lying across his thighs was a weight Jason accepted with pleasure. Jim, a fiftyish man trying to regain the use of his arms and legs after a bout of meningitis, found it far more enjoyable to throw a ball for Aspen, the golden retriever, than to do a certain number of lifts on a machine. And patients trying to regain the use of their speech could practice by giving commands to a dog and were not inclined to lose their temper if the dog did not understand; they knew the dog was not being deliberately obtuse, as they sometimes accused people of being.

"What we've noticed," a staff member at a rehabilitation hospital was quoted as saying in a newspaper interview, "is that the motivation and the performance of the patients increase when they're working with animals." Often an accident or stroke victim is too depressed by the enormity of what has happened to want to make any effort. A woman whose left arm was paralyzed by a stroke claimed it was simply impossible to move it, a claim she forgot when Grizzly visited and she reached to pet him—with her left arm. Another stroke victim who could neither move her left arm nor speak refused to try to pet Grizzly, but when he was placed on an adjacent bed, she did manage to mouth three sentences to him, which the speech therapist applauded as a breakthrough. And a third stroke patient raised his head from his pillow for the first time in order to get a better look at Grizzly, and he too petted the dog with an arm he had hitherto been unable to move. A cowboy lying inert and staring at the ceiling after being thrown by a bull in a rodeo turned on his side and curled around a Doberman when she climbed up beside him. A handler approached a man who day after day sat in a wheelchair and stared at a wallpaper book. The handler's dog put her head on the book and the handler said, "Pretty dog, pretty dog," and the man, who had not spoken since the start of his illness, repeated, "Pretty dog."

Children born with multiple handicaps are sometimes as locked away from the world as comatose patients. Such was the case with Nathan, a small child who could neither see nor hear and who reacted with screams of fright when the unknown invaded his dark and silent world. But when the unknown was the large, silky, softly breathing body of Aspen, Nathan's fists opened and for forty-five minutes, while the dog lay quietly, Nathan trusted enough to explore the feel of the dog's fur.

Another small boy at a school for the deaf and blind, Richard by name, was mentally and physically incapable of communicating and spent his days lying on the floor, his sightless eyes turned to the ceiling. Occasionally he had terrific temper tantrums, and on one such morning, after his parents left him at the school, he screamed nonstop in a frenzy that had the teachers and the other children distraught. Then Aspen and his handler arrived. Aspen went straight to little Richard, licked away a few tears, and settled down beside him. As Richard's bony hands rummaged in Aspen's fur, his screams died away and peace returned to the room.

Debbie Nozawa, a teacher of children with special needs, uses her therapy dog, Cassi, to help her students learn about the world. To teach language concepts such as "same and different," the children place a treat by the object that is the same as the example and say, "Cassi, find the same!" To teach prepositions, a doggie obstacle course is fashioned and the children give Cassi commands: "Go over. Go under. Go around."

But her favorite experience with Cassi, Debbie says, was with PJ, a four-year-old whose congenital brain malformation rendered him blind, deaf, and with spastic cerebral palsy. "Cassi lay perfectly still in the middle of our busy classroom while PJ explored her with his senses of touch and smell and taste. The look on PJ's face as he nestled into Cassi's thick fur, then paused to take in the experience, will stay with me forever. But even more exciting was PJ's response when we put him in his wheelchair, gave him Cassie's leash to hold, and had Cassi pull the wheelchair down the hall. We had tried so hard to get some kind—any kind—of communication from PJ without success. But when I stopped Cassi and asked PJ to tell me if he wanted 'more,' he bobbed his head excitedly. Such a little thing—a head bob. But such a powerful communication for a powerful motivator!"

For children with multiple handicaps, contact with a therapy animal may provide just enough sensory stimulation to encourage them to explore the external world. If nothing else, it at least allays their anxiety about animals. A blind little girl was originally so afraid of animals that she had to be removed from the classroom when the dogs were scheduled to visit, but eventually she came to the doorway. She liked to talk to the handlers, and allowed the dogs to get reasonably near, but scurried off if she sensed one getting too close. One of the handlers decided on a bold step. She snuggled the little girl down in her lap, held her close and talked reassuringly to her, and then took her hand and stroked the dog. Within moments, the little girl was prattling enthusiastically about how she couldn't wait to tell her mother about her new accomplishment.

The problem with a boy named Brad was his lack of motivation to improve his motor skills. Brad had limited vision but acute hearing, and when the handler dropped a dog biscuit into a coffee tin, he was curious enough about the sound to reach in and feel the biscuit. The handler encouraged him to grasp the biscuit, retrieve it from the tin, and hold it out to the dog. That the dog happily took the treat from him each time motivated Brad to continue with this game and thus work on his motor skills without being in the least aware that that was what he was doing.

If dogs can be of such benefit in the lives of handicapped children, should the family with a disabled child consider acquiring one? It depends on the child and the family, of course, but if it does seem like a good idea, the family can contact an agency that specializes in providing service dogs. Such dogs are highly trained to lie still, to accept handling, to walk on a lead without pulling, and to respond immediately to a command, accomplishments that may not be in the family dog's repertoire. With some exceptions in the case of an instinctively nurturing dog, it is probably best to leave animal therapy to therapy-trained dogs.

11
Love, Patience, Acceptance, and Gentleness

GRIZZLY LOVES ME NO MATTER WHAT I DO, six-year-old Harry laboriously printed over his drawing of what purported to be a dog. Harry was in residential treatment in a children's group home, where he did everything possible to get himself ostracized. Not an attractive child to begin with, like other troubled children who come to fear and distrust people, Harry kept people at a distance by wetting and soiling himself and blowing his nose on his clothes. He kicked people for no reason, and burst into violence without warning—except when Grizzly came to visit. Then Harry mellowed out. He knelt on the floor beside Griz and kissed and petted him, and Grizzly, undistracted by the boy's surface disorder, responded with affection and acceptance to the frightened child buried deep within. He listened to the words whispered in his ear and answered with woofs of understanding and encouragement that, in a matter of months and against all odds, persuaded the child that he, Harry, was worth loving. From then on, Harry could be in a room without making everyone else in it wish to murder him.

In writing a review of the service the Good Shepherd volunteers performed, the supervisor of the group home described how her charges reacted when the dogs were visiting:

> These emotionally troubled and behaviorally disordered children—who have suffered multiple abuses—look and act happy, connected, and peaceful, just like so-called "normal" kids. [It is immensely important] for these kids to "fit in," feel that they're "okay" and that they "belong," and to experience pleasure without the threat or fear of abuse. The animals provide a relationship that meets all these needs.
>
> The animals are nonthreatening, nonintimidating, nonintrusive, and they don't project personal problems, expectations, or worries onto the children. Consequently, I have seen children engage in meaningful interactions with the animals, empowering the children and enhancing their sense of self. The animal–child bond is magical, powerful, and corrective!

And the bond is surprisingly lasting. Mandy was another unprepossessing child with a runny nose and thick glasses. Molested sexually from the time she was a baby, Mandy exhibited inappropriate behavior and sexually acted out in the group home. In therapy sessions, her body was present but her mind was absent, a consequence of the sexual abuse she had coped with by fantasizing herself elsewhere. With Grizzly in a therapy session, Mandy focused on his genitals. Lana tried to redirect her behavior by saying such things as, "Grizzly likes it if you pet him between his ears," and rewarding her with praise and a woof from Grizzly when her behavior became more appropriate. Mandy grew to love Grizzly and called him her best friend, a friend she felt safe and happy with.

Too damaged emotionally to be placed in a foster home, when Mandy grew past the age at which she could continue living at the group home, she was transferred to another institution. It happened that a couple of years later, Lana took Grizzly on a visit to that institution. Mandy spotted them in the hall and shouted, "Griz!"

The therapist with Lana murmured, "The girl has an imaginary pal she calls Griz."

"But this *is* Griz," Lana countered, "and she's Mandy. Griz used to visit her at the group home."

It turned out that Mandy had been saying all along that a dog named Griz lived in her room, and the staff assumed that Griz was a creature in her make-believe world. The truth was that in the only place she could call her own—her little room—Mandy had brought love into it by imagining Grizzly there.

Gwen was another child living at the group home, having been removed from her mother's care and placed in the custody of the state while her mother underwent therapy. Because her mother had beaten her whenever the child got the least bit dirty, Gwen had to be perfect. She was afraid to touch anything, not just toys and utensils but another person, and would not allow herself to be hugged. It took several sessions before she could be persuaded that Grizzly was clean and that she would not get into trouble by being in the same room with him. Sitting near and watching other children wash his face and put their blankets over him was all she would do for some time, but one day Gwen reached out and stroked Grizzly for a second. The next time she managed to pet him for a few seconds before jerking her hand away as though it had hit a live wire. The therapist asked how she felt about touching the dog and suggested that Gwen whisper her answer in Grizzly's ear. Grizzly listened and woofled thoughtfully in response. Intrigued, Gwen continued to confide in the dog and Grizzly became the intermediary between Gwen and the therapist, with Lana acting as Grizzly's translator. The therapist would say, "Gwen, tell Grizzly what it was like when the boy hit you." Gwen whispered, Grizzly said, "Woof, woof," and Lana translated: "Grizzly says he's glad you told him about that."

Word came that Gwen's mother had regained custody of her child, a piece of news so upsetting to Gwen that she was unable to sleep the night before her mother was due to come for her. Lana was visiting with Grizzly that day, and she and the therapist decided just to let Gwen be with Grizzly this last time. They sat quietly beside the child, and soon Gwen fell asleep on the floor with her arms around Grizzly's neck.

Her mother arrived and was shown to the room. "What are you doing with that dirty dog!" she screamed. "Get away from that filthy creature!"

Gwen and Grizzly scrambled to their feet, and Gwen protested, "Grizzly's clean. He's my best friend."

"He's mean! Anyone can see he's mean." And, indeed, Grizzly had slowly moved forward to stand between the child and her mother.

"He's wonderful," Gwen protested, putting her arms around Grizzly's neck. "He loves me."

"Get away from him. Where are your clothes? We'll have to change your dress."

"I don't want to go with you!"

But Gwen had no choice because her mother was armed with a court order. Lana told Grizzly to downstay, while Gwen's mother grasped the child's arm and yanked her from the room. Times like this are the downside for handlers doing animal-assisted therapy, when they witness helpless children having to return to situations that were so wounding to them in the first place.

This happened with a Native American child whom a doctor brought to a Salt Lake City hospital, not just for treatment of her epileptic seizures but because her bruised body gave evidence of physical abuse. The little girl did not speak English and was frightened of everyone and everything in the hospital—except for Grizzly. She opened her eyes and hugged him when he lay beside her, and she learned to speak one word in the hospital: "Griz." But Lana and Grizzly could not build on the relationship because after her seizures were stabilized and her bruises healed, the little girl had to be returned to the reservation.

On still another occasion, Lana and Grizzly had been working with a six-year-old named Douglas for some time in a group home when he began a session by running to Grizzly with "some really bad news" to tell him: his birth mother, from whose care he had been removed when he was three, was coming to take him away. He told Grizzly that it was going to be hard to leave him and that he wished Griz could come with him to his new home. Grizzly whined and vocalized, and when Douglas asked what he was saying, Lana told him that Griz was probably saying he was sad that Douglas would be leaving but that he understood it was important for him to go and he was happy for him that he would get to be in a family. She added that if Douglas wrote Grizzly a letter, Grizzly would smell his scent and know that he was doing all right. As though in corroboration, Grizzly sniffed Douglas at that point.

Lana brought out a brush, shedding blade, and soft bristled brush, and while Douglas groomed Grizzly, he began to talk about the family he had been taken from three years before: his teenage brother and sister, his mother, and the father who had divorced his mother. He observed wistfully that he wished his father had stayed with the family and kept it together, and he speculated about what it would be like when he went back now. He asked if he could taste one of Grizzly's dog biscuits and said he wished he could be a dog and be taken care of like Grizzly.

Another boy who wished he was a dog began acting out the wish, getting down on all fours and barking and asking to be petted and putting Grizzly's leash and collar around his own neck. Born to a severely disturbed mother, Alan was a shell of a child. He looked like an okay kid who smiled real smiles but behind the facade churned a dark fantasy world of killing and maiming. He was extraordinarily handsome, which made him appealing, but his therapist described him to Lana as "the type of person who can grin charmingly while he thinks about how to hurt you."

The goal of therapy with Alan, Lana was told, was to try to break through the facade to the inner region where Alan really existed, no easy task because the boy readily did everything he was asked, like giving hugs, but he was not there doing it; he just went through the motions wearing a pretend smile. The only time he seemed engaged at all was when he was playing at being a dog. Lana pointed out to him that Grizzly knew perfectly well that

Alan was not a dog and would only respond to him if he did human things, not dog things, and she reinforced every bit of behavior that went with being a child.

Little by little, over a period of two years, Alan developed a healthy relationship with Grizzly, acting not like a fellow animal but a boy with a dog. He walked him and talked to him and learned to recognize when the dog was happy, sad, tired, or hungry. Lana made a strong point of this in an effort to teach Alan to connect his mind and body. He learned to put water in a bowl and bring it to Grizzly, who rewarded him with talk and a muzzle kiss. His relationship with Grizzly became the first real connection Alan had ever had with any living creature. To some extent, it carried over to his therapist. In their individual sessions he showed some genuine feeling and occasionally established eye contact, although the eye contact sometimes scared him and he broke it off abruptly.

After two years Alan went to live with a foster family. He loved being in a family and hoped he would be adopted, but four months later he was back in the treatment center, his pretend smile firmly in place. The threat of intimacy and attachment had been too much for him. He had exploded and threatened to kill his foster mother and father and their children, and he had been violent toward neighborhood kids, pushing, tripping, kicking, and hitting them.

"When he came back," his therapist told Lana, "he asked me to write a letter for him to his own mother, saying, 'I had a family for four and a half months.' He knows exactly how long he was there. He knows the hours of each day and what activity happens each day. I think it's how he keeps a kind of order in his life. He's bright and he's beautiful and he's very intelligent, and he breaks your heart because he shows potential for attachment and genuine affection but it is not something he can sustain. He did it for a while with Grizzly, but he may be a kid who cannot ever be in a family because he's been too traumatized."

When Alan came into the therapy room after he returned to the center and saw Grizzly there, instead of greeting him with pleasure, he said, "Oh, I thought he was dead." Alan's voice was flat. His eyes roamed the room blankly, and he picked up toys at random and immediately put them down again. Lana realized with dismay that they were back at square one; Alan's connection with the world had been severed, even his connection with Grizzly. Interestingly enough, Grizzly seemed to realize it too. Instead of attempting to engage Alan, Grizzly wandered aimlessly around the room, mirroring Alan's own distanced behavior.

Because Alan turned eight shortly after that and the residence was for children aged two to seven, Alan went to another placement and Lana and Grizzly did not see him again. But Lana often thought about him and wondered what the future held for him. A ghastly fact in his early history was that he had watched his sadistic father wring the neck of a neighbor's cat and seen him skin animals alive. As Albert Schweitzer once observed, "Anyone who has accustomed himself to regard the life of *any* living creature as worthless is in danger of arriving also at the idea of worthless human lives." Alan had been introduced to the idea of violence and the worthlessness of lives early in his own life, and it was not hard to imagine him growing up to be a killer. But Lana hoped that having had Grizzly as the strongest attachment in his life, Alan might come to value other animals and, in the reverse of Dr. Schweitzer's dictum, learn through them to value human lives as well.

In addition to whatever specific good an individual therapy animal might do for a child, a general goal for The Good Shepherd Association was to lead people to appreciate animals in general and family pets in particular, to look at them with different eyes and understand their physical and emotional needs. Long ago human beings domesticated dogs and cats, and by doing so, became responsible for them, which means they do not deserve to be discarded when their presence becomes inconvenient or they become ill or old. They are not living exhibits to enlighten children about the birth process and then be thrown away. Nor are they to be treated as animate alarm systems, to be chained outside night and day to give warning when strangers approach.

A woman who owned a German shepherd took the dog to a grooming establishment and asked to have all his fur shaved off because she could not abide his shedding. The distressed groomer asked Lana to talk to the owner, which she did, explaining that the dog would have both health and psychological problems if his coat were removed. He would be as humiliated as the woman herself would be at being forced to go outside naked, and he would be no less vulnerable than she to injury and the effects of sun and wind. Far more to the point, Lana said, would be improving the dog's coat by seeing that his nutrition was optimal and brushing him daily to remove loose hairs. That plus vacuuming the rugs in the house frequently would pretty much take care of the problem, and if some stray hairs did appear on the furniture, that was a very small price to pay when weighed against the pleasure a well-cared-for dog and valued companion could be.

Because she suspected that the woman tied the dog outside a good deal of the time, Lana described a house she passed each day where the dog was chained in a gravel driveway in the direct sun even though there were shade trees nearby. Day in, day out, year following year, he was chained there, not allowed to run loose even when the children in the family were playing in the yard. "Dogs are pack animals," Lana said. "The family they belong to is their pack, and they need to be with them. If they are not with them and don't have a chance to learn human rules, they will follow dog rules, and that can mean barking and biting and perhaps an unwanted viciousness." Lana did not know whether she had persuaded this woman to take more thoughtful care of her animal, but she did hear from the groomer that the dog was being brought in monthly for grooming and there was no more talk of shaving off his fur.

On one of their biweekly visits to Arden, Lana picked up the fact that Arden was having a lot of trouble with relationships, and she suggested to Mark that she bring not only Grizzly to the next session but Kodyella and Bayley, a new puppy they had gotten from Ella. This would give them a reason to discuss, and perhaps illustrate, issues that Arden was having problems with. Arden was thrilled with the idea of meeting Grizzly's dog family and she was waiting at the door when Lana arrived, along with Dave, who was acting that day as the handler for Kodyella. Lana handed Bayley's leash to Arden, and she proudly guided the puppy to the therapy room, where they all settled down, Kodyella protectively near Bayley. For an hour, Arden had the chance to observe mother, father, and youngster. She saw how Kodyella protected Bayley and taught him rules.

One rule for a puppy is to respect his elders and not walk up into the face of a male. "If Bayley doesn't learn this rule," Lana explained to Arden, "he will be bitten. That's what parents do. They teach their children the rules so they will be safe."

"And that's what the staff here does," Mark elaborated. "Kodyella nips Bayley to teach him not to barge into Grizzly's space, and the staff disciplines you to teach you the rules so you won't get hurt for breaking them."

Lana added, "Kodyella disciplines Bayley with love, and when he follows the rules, he gets a muzzle kiss from Grizzly as a reward."

"There are rewards for children who follow the rules," Mark pointed out. "People like you better when they can count on your behavior to be appropriate and when you give them the space they need. Look at the dogs. They're not all over each other. They're keeping their mouths and their paws to themselves."

"Kodyella and Grizzly have taught Bayley a proper distance and respect," Lana said. "They are lenient about letting him play because play is healthy for a puppy—it's his way of learning about the world—but they discipline him at the same time."

"Do they love him?" Arden asked.

"They love him and they love each other. They wake up every morning and greet each other with muzzle kisses. Animals are not as afraid as we human beings are of showing their love."

All through the hour, Arden watched the dogs and asked questions. It was safe to talk about the dogs. She could discuss behavior without its being *her* behavior up for criticism, and she could draw conclusions without its being adults handing down "shoulds." The adults in the room knew she was absorbing, learning, weighing, thinking, and they were happy to pretend that all they were talking about was the animal family.

Afterward, Mark thanked Lana and Dave for bringing the dogs and said he had an idea that the visit would prove to be important for Arden. Commenting on the value of animal-assisted therapy in general, he speculated that it was due to several factors: the neutral ground the dogs provided, their role as go-betweens, the atmosphere of acceptance, and the fact that they had no agenda of their own and their motives could not be doubted. "They are like a conduit through which feelings can flow from person to person," was how Mark put it. He added, "I don't know what the dogs get out of it, but I hope they get some satisfaction in return for all the good they do."

All the handlers were certain that the dogs got a great deal out of their therapy visits. Nothing else would account for how a dog danced with excitement when the therapy bag came out of the hall closet. Paulette recalled how Onyx had started out in life not liking people and being afraid of other dogs, but now she happily pulled a wagon filled with children and dragged Paulette over to little ones on her belly, which is the way she had learned to approach small children. Several of the therapy dogs tended to be incorrigible at home, doing such things as stealing and eating whole loaves of bread, appropriating books from tables and carrying them into the backyard, and "re-landscaping" entire flower beds. One dog had even taken all the dirty dishes out of the sink, including three glass cereal bowls, polished them spotless, and left them neatly lined up—and unbroken—on the kitchen floor. But when the dogs went to work, they were models of decorum: They made themselves into unmoving pillows for a child to lie against, climbed delicately on a bed to be with a fragile person, or paced slowly with a toddler.

One handler, owner of a dog who was mischievous at home, marveled that her dog never needed to be corrected for misbehavior when she was in a therapy situation but always seemed to understand the rules and what was expected of her. The dog had even allowed a group of children to give her a bath, to soap and rinse her while she stood perfectly still and did not shake even once. At home, on the other hand, the dog was quite given to ignoring the rules about not getting on the furniture, not rooting around in the garbage, and not swiping food off the kitchen counter.

Cats, too, seemed to sense the difference between home and work. Judy Mills took her prize-winning Persian, now retired from competition, to the bedside of a dying woman who, as it happened, had often judged him in cat shows. As Judy described it, "I placed Cody on the bed beside her and gently rested her hand on the cat's head and neck. Margie softly moved her fingers as if to bury them in his coat. Cody broke into purrs so loud that his cheeks filled with air. Then, totally unprompted by me, he laid his throat against the back of her hand so that Margie could feel his purr, and he stayed there until it was time to leave. I am so glad he brought her comfort before she died."

When Lana hit a plateau with an emotionally disturbed child she had been working with for a year, she asked Judy to bring Cody to the sessions. The little boy was terrified of cats, but within a surprisingly short time Cody won him over and soon he was burying his face in Cody's luxuriant fur and confiding secrets he had been unable to express to the therapist or any other person. Cody and Grizzly co-treated, and how well they worked together as a team was a revelation. They had not known each other before they were brought together to heal this child, and their partnership and the mutual love and respect they showed each other suggested to both Lana and Judy how much there is still to learn from and about animals.

What allows an animal to discriminate between behavior at home and behavior at work? Is it intelligence? In Lana's opinion, animals are smarter than we are in some ways about how to live in this world, how to adapt. "We need to stop measuring intelligence in animals based on our understanding of what we think intelligence is. If we couldn't scent down a rabbit, dogs measuring our intelligence would decide we were pretty dumb. Rather than getting hung up on the question of how bright or dumb animals are, let's learn what they have to teach us, starting with love, patience, acceptance, and gentleness."

A letter to the editor appearing in the November 22, 1993, issue of *Newsweek* bears on this subject:

> Elizabeth Marshall Thomas is right on—and beautifully so—in making a case for the existence of dog consciousness in her book *The Hidden Life of Dogs.* I'm a psychologist, and for the past 22 years I have had dogs work with kids in psychoanalytic play-therapy and kept dogs in the office during sessions with adults. Kids will tell dogs things they wouldn't dream of telling humans, and gain comfort in the process. Troll, a Lab, could spot a paranoid personality within minutes (and would hide under the desk). Dogs instinctively know what people need and supply the correct emotional response—hard to imagine unless we assume they have some kind of thought process and inner life.

Mother Teresa once observed: "In this life we cannot do great things. We can only do small things with great love." Volunteering is a small thing, but the handlers in The Good Shepherd Association do it with love. Asked what keeps them motivated to do a job with no monetary rewards and very little recognition, they give an assortment of answers, among them the following:

> This has been the most incredibly rewarding experience of my life. Hawkeye has changed the way I look at children, and changed the way I look at life. Different things are important to me now—simple things and brief miraculous moments, like the hug and "I love you, Hawkeye" a little boy gives each time we say goodbye. And the pride in that same boy's face when he walks past his friends with his therapy dog heeling by his side. This is why I volunteer. I know Hawkeye is making a difference in someone's life. With my assistance, he is

making the world a better place. And what could be more important than that?

—Karen Schroyer

When I am working with one of my animals, I feel that I serve as a channel through which my animal teammate, the individuals I serve, and my fellow volunteers may receive spiritual, emotional, and educational support in a way that makes them feel respected, lovable, and capable.

—Debbie Nozawa

I like to witness the miracle of the human–animal bond—something that happens when they connect. To me, a "big" miracle (something permanently life-changing or life-saving) is not the point. What keeps me going is the little miracle of that direct-connect experience—I like to see others feel what I feel when I'm with my dogs.

—Grace Whitaker

The steps are sometimes small but the rewards are big. I am so happy to share the unconditional love of my teammate. I believe that, for every person's life we can change in a positive manner, we will feel blessed. I also believe that, through volunteering with my dog, I am helping to educate the public about the positive power of the human–animal bond and helping to create an environment of nurturing for those with special needs.

—Betty Brown

My cat Cody is really an "angel in a kitty suit." I can't stress enough how much gratification I have gotten by sharing something I love so much with a child in need, by helping in the healing process, and by demonstrating to the community something all of us already know, and that is that animals really are the best therapists.

—Judy Mills

The handlers leave a facility feeling elated and full of self-worth because it is impossible to give away unconditional love and acceptance without getting some back. The animals make it possible for human beings to reach out to one another. Without them as intermediaries, people are cautious about reacting to a stranger, but let the approach be through a tail-wagging dog or a purring cat and inhibitions melt, positive regard springs up, smiles become genuine. There is caring and warmth in the atmosphere, and everyone feels the better for it.

12
So Much More That Hasn't Ended

Lana and Grizzly had been working with Arden for three years when they were invited to a dinner honoring volunteers at the residential treatment center. Because she had made a mistake in the time, Lana was twenty minutes late in arriving, and Arden, who had obviously been afraid she was not coming, rushed to greet her, relief and welcome written full on her face. When she saw the girl, Lana came close to doing a comic double-take, for the ugly duckling, although not quite a swan, looked almost grown-up and amazingly attractive. She was dressed in a black skirt and sweater, nylon stockings, and heels. Her hair shone, her polished nails gleamed, and she wore a slight hint of makeup. She grinned when she saw Lana's look of surprise and surprised her still more by reaching out hesitantly to give her a hug.

Preparations for the dinner had been going on for days. With some help from the staff, the children had made tablecloths, place cards, and centerpieces for each table and planned and cooked a dinner of spaghetti, green salad, cheese, and fruit. They had even concocted a variety of desserts, including their own favorite—cheesecake. After dinner the children entertained with songs. The musician in Lana was surprised and pleased to find they actually sang on pitch, which in her experience was highly unusual in children. When it came the turn of the older kids, Arden's group sang "*Lean on Me*," bringing tears to Lana's eyes. While the song continued, the children went out in the audience and took the hand of the volunteer they were thanking. Arden led Grizzly and Lana on stage and there they stood, surrounded by children who sang like angels but who had lived in hell most of their short lives.

The children ranged in age from five to seventeen, and when the singing was over, the little ones were anxious to pet and hug Grizzly. Arden was generous about sharing "her dog," even to the extent of having him lie down and "talk" to three of the smallest children. She knew they needed to be close and warm, just as she had needed it when Grizzly first came to her. When Grizzly was tired of talking, she buckled him into his harness, attached a long lead on the D ring, and strung seven children on the line so they could all go for a walk with Griz.

Lana described the evening to Dave and spoke with pleasure of all the changes she could see in Arden. Arden had come a long way from the untidy, unruly, frequently out-of-control child she had been, but Lana was aware of just how fragile Arden still was and wondered what would happen to her when she became too old to stay on at the residence. She would step out of the supportive, protected environment of the group home into an indifferent world, with no family to give her shelter, no friends to take her by the hand. The thought haunted Lana and she returned to it again and again.

What happened to adolescents when the custodial role of the state came to an end? There should be some sort of halfway house, Lana thought, a place of safety, a home base for them, perhaps a place in the country. Yes, certainly a place in the country so they did not step out alone onto city streets. Voluntary? Yes, voluntary, by all means, because other people had been making decisions for them all their lives and this decision to take shelter until, like a butterfly, their wings dried and they could make their way in the world, must be their own. Free? They would have no money but their steps to independence would be undermined if it was just one more shelter the state provided, which meant that it would have to be a place of work . . . working . . . a working farm.

A working farm. Lana liked the sound of it. It was a familiar phrase. But not to her. She knew little about the economics of a farm. What she knew were therapy animals. And what did eighteen-year-olds coming out of residential homes know? The mentors in their lives had all been therapists and teachers. They had not observed adults following a variety of professions. What they knew were psychotherapists, speech therapists, art therapists, music therapists. Suppose the work of the farm were to be therapy? Therapy for and with animals? Yes! And again yes! said Lana's heart and mind.

She went on dreaming. The farm would be a place where institutionalized adolescents could learn skills to help them prepare for independence: animal caretaking, grooming, and training skills. A variety of animals would populate the farm: horses and other farm animals; dogs and cats, of course; even injured wildlife in need of refuge. A training center for therapy and companion animals might be established. Perhaps, in line with a program already being tried out in Washington State, the initial training of therapy animals could be done by women in prison and then continued and refined at the farm. Sick or injured animals would be treated and unwanted animals trained for adoption; the animals that came to them would be rehabilitated, never sold or slaughtered.

The farm would be a setting with trees and pastureland, a tranquil place where outpatients could come. There would be animal-assisted therapy for the emotionally troubled, schooling in the use of service dogs for the wheelchair-bound and the blind, horseback riding for the physically disabled. The adolescents living at the farm would participate in the training of both the service dogs and the therapy animals. They could also help train dogs and their handlers to visit facilities in the community to deliver animal-assisted therapy.

Early on, Lana had served on a Delta Society task force making a comprehensive analysis of educational needs in the field of animal-assisted therapy and was well aware that the biggest challenge in the field was to standardize training. This was a necessary first step toward the ultimate goal of having animal-assisted therapy become a paraprofession, comparable to art or music or physical therapy, with courses of study at the college level culminating in the granting of a degree, which would be followed by a license to practice.

Lana longed to be strongly involved in taking the field in this direction; what better way than to set up a model training facility? And while she was dreaming, why not add a research library specializing in material about animal-assisted therapy and the human–animal bond?

But she was only dreaming. As executive director, she had The Good Shepherd Association to run. In just four years, from 1992 to 1996, the organization had grown from a few people to dozens of handler and animal teams working in caregiving facilities in and around Salt Lake City. Dave's fund-raising efforts had been amazingly successful, resulting in a substantial nest egg for the organization. Lana, Grizzly, and some others had been featured twice on national television, while Grizzly's story was spotlighted in *Reader's Digest*. The organization was becoming increasingly professional, with a small paid staff, rigorous standards, and public accountability.

But the very success of the organization was causing problems. A number of members regretted the professionalization of the service and wished to return to being a clublike organization held together by a core group of dedicated volunteers. Paulette Bethel and several other people resigned over this philosophical split, with considerable emotional fallout. Members of the Board of Directors began to take sides, with key members of the board refusing to communicate with Lana. Because Lana and Grizzly were the main focus of media attention, jealousy and mistrust over her prominence became rife, and increasingly she became the subject of criticism and suspicion.

According to Peter Van Hook, a consultant specializing in working with troubled nonprofit organizations, what was operating here was the "Founder Syndrome." In his description, founders of non-profit organizations like The Good Shepherd Association tend to be single-minded visionaries dedicated to seeing that the mission for which the organization was established is being carried out. More often than not, the founders are not good administrators and do not have much interest in, or talent for, performing administrative tasks, so they tend to leave the executive part of their job to others. Unfortunately, it is in these executive tasks where the power and authority in an organization ultimately reside.

In the case of The Good Shepherd Association, Lana concentrated on training and program development, leaving financial management, personnel issues, and operating policies and procedures to others. With Lana focused on service delivery and Dave on fund-raising, they were blind to the dynamics of the organization, and others moved to take control. Dave resigned from the board in protest, and following bitter controversy, in 1997 the board voted to fire Lana and rename the organization. Suddenly The Good Shepherd Association was no more.

Five years of Lana's life and Dave's, her vision and his fund-raising efforts, had gone into the organization. It seemed almost unthinkable that they had been ousted, and not only ousted but made the targets of considerable anger and villification. But that too was part of the Founder Syndrome, Peter Van Hook told them, and he wryly quoted the maxim, "No good deed goes unpunished."

"You dedicated your lives to this thing and gave it everything you had," he said. "Now you have to pay for the good you did. It doesn't make sense, but it happens all the time."

That it was a common fate of founders of organizations did not make it any easier for Lana to take. The Good Shepherd Association had been her life, her passion, her connection to the world. Now it had been taken away from her without explanation and without thanks by a small number of individuals acting in secrecy. At an open meeting of the general membership, there were angry demands by many of the volunteers for an explanation of Lana's sudden termination, but no clear reasons were given, nor did any seem to exist. There were hints of financial improprieties, but every effort to have these hints made specific circled around and came to rest each time solely on a three-hundred dollar discrepancy in petty cash at a time two years earlier when the organization was having trouble finding someone to keep the books properly. To use this as a means of discrediting Lana was absurd on the face of it, for not only had she and Dave put considerable amounts of their own money into the organization but Lana was never the person responsible for handling the financial record-keeping.

For a couple of months Lana asked for facts, pleaded for reasons, and tried to understand why, behind the scenes, efforts were being made to destroy her reputation with agencies and service organizations and the media. Then she gave up and sank into a depression that alternated with bouts of rage and feelings of hopelessness. Not since Jeremy's death had she been filled with such despair. Dave watched with deepening concern as he battled with his own feelings of rage over the actions of this small group of people and the hurt that had resulted for so many. Even Grizzly seemed at a loss as to what to do. He wandered around the house aimlessly, unable to understand why Lana wasn't taking him to visit his charges.

But friends like Betty Brown, Judy Mills, Grace Whitaker, Debbie Nozawa, and Karen Schroyer were determined to rally Lana. They would not let her give up on the work. They insisted on meeting, along with Dave and Betty's husband, Bob, to chart a course to keep the dream of a professional animal-assisted therapy organization alive. Constituting themselves the nucleus of a new organization and determined not to repeat the mistakes of the past, they worked out safeguards to insure that the new organization would be based on a shared set of values, on open and honest communication, on a clearly articulated set of ethical standards, and on a commitment to the very highest quality of service.

When Lana refused to consider any position of leadership, Betty Brown volunteered to assume the responsibility, with the understanding that she would be able to draw on Lana's experience and expertise. Dave agreed to act as chairman of the new governing board and undertook to draft articles of incorporation and a set of bylaws that mandated board accountability to the membership such that a takeover like the one they had gone through could not happen again. He also drew up the papers necessary to register the organization as a tax-exempt charity with the IRS.

Judy Mills designed a logo with a stylized dog, cat, and child sitting together, looking to a far horizon. The dog was Grizzly, the cat was Cody, and the child was the boy they had worked with so closely and successfully. The remaining problem was a name for the organization. After trying and discarding several, they settled on Utah Animal-Assisted Therapy Association as the name most descriptive of the purpose of the organization and its commitment to professionalism.

The UAATA, following a strategy of careful growth, is slowly building a core group of volunteers and a solid board committed to achieving the goals that have been set out. Dave has already secured several foundation grants to help them meet their basic expenses while they expand their services. Currently, all the staff members are volunteers and all, with the exception of Lana, hold full-time outside jobs. Faced once more with the problem of picking up the pieces of her life, Lana decided to return to the University of Utah. She graduated with a BS degree in June 1998 and plans to go to graduate school to further her studies.

Not in the least forgotten is her dream of a "therapeutic farm." It is the cornerstone of UAATA's vision for the future. Tentatively titled Aesop's Stables, it will be modeled after Green Chimneys, a therapeutic farm and residential treatment program located about fifty miles north of New York City. "Because we do not have a large city to draw from the way Green Chimneys does," Dave says, "we probably won't be able to grow in the same way. But grow we shall because the need is as great here in the West as it is back East, and we are absolutely committed to making the dream of Aesop's Stables a reality."

The logistical issues and, in particular, the funding required for such a project keep the farm only a misty vision for the time being. But sometimes, when she can take time from her studies,

Lana wanders back roads half expecting that one day she will round a curve or come over a rise and there it will be: the place of her dreams. Grizzly, seat belt firmly buckled, rides along on the front seat beside her, as years before he rode beside Jeremy in Jeremy's little blue pickup, and Lana shares her thoughts with him as Jeremy once did.

"How far we've come, Grizzly," she ruminated one afternoon as they poked along a byroad. "How much we've come through. I didn't think we'd make it sometimes. Sometimes I didn't think it was worth trying to keep on trying." She was silent for a bit. "I read something the other day. 'If something ends,' a poet wrote to another poet, 'still, how infinitely much more there is that isn't ending.' We've found that out, haven't we, Griz, you and I? A couple of times so much has ended for us, but still there turns out to be so much more that hasn't ended. What are you saying, that you always knew that? You're a wise dog, Griz."

Does Grizzly remember Jeremy? His ears prick forward whenever Lana mentions Jeremy's name, and when, not so long ago, she took him on a visit to Oregon and asked him to find Jeremy's grave, he circled the cemetery until he came to it.

"Of course," said Ella matter-of-factly when Lana marveled that, eight years after Jeremy's death, Grizzly could still go to his boy's headstone and lie down by it. "He's a German shepherd." And no anecdote Lana told her about Grizzly's part in the work they had done together surprised her. "It's Grizzly's job," she explained. "No, more than that, it's his *profession.* It is what he was put in the world to do—to be the good shepherd."

And Lana? Was it the work she was put in the world to do? Perhaps Jeremy had glimpsed it when he said, "Mom, I want you to have Grizzly. Maybe you and he can do something to help other sick kids." And perhaps, just perhaps, it was why Grizzly had so insistently encouraged her to keep on living. He knew that the two of them had work to do.

How You Can Help

The Utah Animal-Assisted Therapy Association welcomes all who want to lend a helping hand (or paw). No matter where you live, you can support the work being carried on by Lana, Grizzly, and their colleagues by sending a tax-exempt donation to:

Utah Animal-Assisted Therapy Association
P.O. Box 18771
Salt Lake City, UT 84118-8771
Telephone: 801-963-7696 Fax: 801-963-7676
E-mail: info@uaata.org
Web site: http://www.uaata.org

UAATA is a tax-exempt 501(c)(3) charitable organization.

For more information on animal-assisted therapy, service dogs for people with disabilities, and the health benefits of companion animals, contact Delta Society at (800) 869-6898, visit the Web site www.deltasociety.org, or order a complimentary booklet by e-mail from orderit@paragongroup.com.